LEADING INNOVATION

5 Steps to Monetising Ideas for Business Growth

Tracy Walsh

First published by OMNE Publishing in 2016

National Library of Australia Cataloguing-in-Publication entry
Creator: Walsh, Tracy, author.
Title: Leading Innovation: 5 Steps to Monetising Ideas for Business Growth
ISBN: 9780994425553 (pbk.)
Subjects: Leadership--Management.
Leadership--Australia--Management.
Innovation in business--Australia.

Dewey Number: 658.42

Disclaimer

The material in this publication is of the nature of general comment only, and does not represent professional advice. It is not intended to provide specific guidance for particular circumstances and it should not be relied on as the basis for any decision to take action or not take action on any matter which it covers. Readers should obtain professional advice where appropriate, before making any such decision. The author and publisher disclaim all responsibility and liability to any person, arising directly or indirectly from any person taking or not taking action based on the information in this publication.

Editing: OMNE Author Solutions
Front Cover, back cover & additional graphics: Designerbility
Layout: OMNE Author Solutions
Printing: OMNE Publishing

The book is available as a print or ebook from all good bookstores, Amazon and the author's website www.corporateinnovationsaustralia.com.au

Dedication

I dedicate this book to my father Michael Walsh (now passed), my mother Heather, sister Kate, and my family (in particular the Walsh cousins). I thank you for supporting my compulsion to share the benefit of my experience and the wisdom of those around me.

Acknowledgements

I would first like to acknowledge my husband, Dr. Wayne Hellmuth (PhD IT Design Science), who took time away from finishing his doctorate to contribute to the Revolutionise chapter.

I thank the prominent executives featured in this book for their time, wisdom and support for my 5-step model. They all have in common the desire to reinvent and carry the flag for innovative workforces. To my peers, former managers and contacts in businesses who persist through an onslaught of change—technological, cultural and structural—I hope this book provides some tools that prove useful with your teams.

Contents

FOREWORD

I began my career as a television journalist and I fundamentally believed then that the public had the right to know – about news, events, decisions, activities – anything that could impact or benefit them. In some way I wanted to add value to the lives of others.

Fresh out of university and a six-month stint at the Nine Network, at the tender age of 21, I jumped in. I moved to country New South Wales, to a town called Taree, where I took up the post of regional news reporter. Far from my family and friends in Brisbane, I knew no-one, but within the week I soon found my way. I began honing my skills for uncovering information and built strong connections that would help me fill my quota of three complete stories to air by 6pm. I learned the importance of collaboration with the Mayor of Taree, council members, police detectives and local sporting heroes. I became adept at diving into issues to learn every scrap of information until it made sense and I could give the people a voice.

I aimed for balanced and fair reporting. In my short skirts and big hair (remember the early 90's?), I felt that I had been given a platform and that it was my duty to reach and inform audiences about the things that mattered most to them.

This ethos has moved with me to the corporate world. Minus the short skirts and big hair, I have felt compelled to facilitate problem solving and communication at all levels to keep workforces informed, involved and motivated. I believe that workers, middle managers and even CEOs need a voice and to be heard. Today, there are pressures at every level and ever increasing distractions. Now more than ever, in these changing times, understanding can only be achieved through effective and regular two-way communication.

Big companies are microcosms of society with distinct rules, structures and cultural norms. This book celebrates business leaders who want to find a better way to hear, recognise and instigate measures to move workforces along the change continuum and into the innovation space. A much better reality exists beyond the constraints of the status quo for corporates and governments and it is achievable through the 5-step Innovation Accelerator method.

INTRODUCTION

Are you pulled in different directions, accountable to everyone and almost paralysed at the thought of adding innovation to the 'to do' list?

Let's put you in the shoes of the Innovative CEO. How do they fit? If you are particularly adept at being all things to all people, they probably fit well. There are vast numbers of people to please – shareholders, regulators, customers, employees, unions, banks, etc. At the same time you are listening, deciding, reporting, saying only the "right" things to the right people – while somehow finding the time to walk the halls, know the ins and outs of daily operations and personally thank your high performing staff. Sound familiar? You are expected to keep one eye on competitors, a hand in improving efficiencies and an ear to the ground for new technologies. To use the term "competing priorities" would be an understatement. Juggling skills would probably prove handy.

To survive in corporate cultures, you must be agile, a risk taker and at the same time intimately knowledgeable about both your people and customers. Demonstrating an even temperament, you are able to deconstruct business models and structures to reinvigorate and reflect a delivery focus. Well connected and open to partnerships, the Innovative CEO can take demoralised teams through change and on the journey to innovation. You can communicate with conviction and clarity what the company vision is and what success looks like without dictating exactly how it should be done.

The Innovative CEO will hand pick innovators, partner with Universities, bring in technical expertise and encourage design thinking within existing teams. You are driven by the challenge of interpreting and better understanding your customer's desires, wants and needs. Then you make business decisions accordingly.

The reality is that the Innovative CEO and today's most successful leaders are one and the same. They know that business survival and contemporary leadership requires out-of-the-box thinking that includes:

- access to emerging technologies
- stronger innovation capabilities
- entry to new markets
- innovation-friendly work cultures
- cultivating workforces that are attuned to the interests of today's global and tech-savvy customers.

Innovation isn't new

Astounding achievements aside, it is important to remember that innovation didn't begin with Steve Jobs. There is a much broader time continuum at play. From the first Etruscans who inked new designs on their clay pots to Elon Musk's recent reinvention of the electric car, innovation is inherent to the human condition. In between we find Egyptian pyramid design and Roman aqueducts.

Each of these capture the zeitgeist or inventive spirit of their ages. There is something that exists in the human spirit; a drive not only to do more but to do better, to improve upon what we have already done. Now more than ever we are equipped with the means to innovate. Digital connectivity has placed information, systems, and ideas from around the world at our fingertips. Progress can now be made in leaps and bounds, not brick by brick.

However, there is another part of the human spirit that a discussion of innovation cannot ignore: a fear of failure. As this book unfolds, you will come to see failure as an important part of the journey.

Innovation need not be 'big bang' moments: it can start small, perhaps with encouraging people to think in new and subtly transformative ways about what they are doing and how they are doing it. It doesn't have to be difficult, but it does demand persistence.

Innovation roadblocks

Some leaders are more comfortable with innovation than others. However, in my experience there are five common barriers to corporate innovation. They are:

Risk aversion – With different comfort levels surrounding risk, board members may be reluctant to take a chance on investing in something that is unproven or new. Alternatively, leadership teams may be averse to taking on innovations that the board favours. There may also be a culture of caution or a lack of capital that prioritises 'business as usual' ahead of innovative projects.

Believing that innovation is optional – There is a surprisingly widespread perception that innovation is simply an appendage, or 'nice to have'. In these situations, leaders who put innovation on the backburner are convinced that current success with a stable full of loyal customers will likewise translate to future success. However, actively ignoring innovation is only viable in the short term. Staying still and sticking only to what you know just isn't feasible or credible in the drive for a sustainable business.

Overwhelm – Since the GFC, there has been significant downsizing, restructuring and outsourcing. In many cases, these changes have been poorly handled, leaving team members disengaged from the organisation and its vision. These team members are unlikely to innovate if their hearts aren't in their jobs and they aren't performing their roles to capacity in the company. There may be a strict hierarchy or even a matrix design in which communication flow isn't effective, which leads to a pronounced disconnect between teams and managers or executive leadership.

Wrong people with wrong skills – There may be a belief that the existing talent in the organisation isn't appropriate for innovation. Those who throw up this roadblock seem to always focus on what the company isn't. For example, you might hear people say that the organisational structure isn't set up for technical innovation. However, as this book will explain, in this day and age, there is a broad and accessible range of resources on offer.

Lack of formal innovation processes – Many companies don't have an innovation strategy. They don't have an innovation function or a governance process for idea expression, management and review. Design thinking may be left to externals or not valued at all.

These roadblocks span financial, cultural, people, process and technology problems, all of which impede the potential for innovation to thrive.

Getting on the right course

In the spirit of problem solving, there are five critical steps, which, when followed, create the conditions needed to make innovation an integral part of business operations.

Fearlessly applying these five steps is the hallmark of forward-thinking companies. If this book does its job, it should give

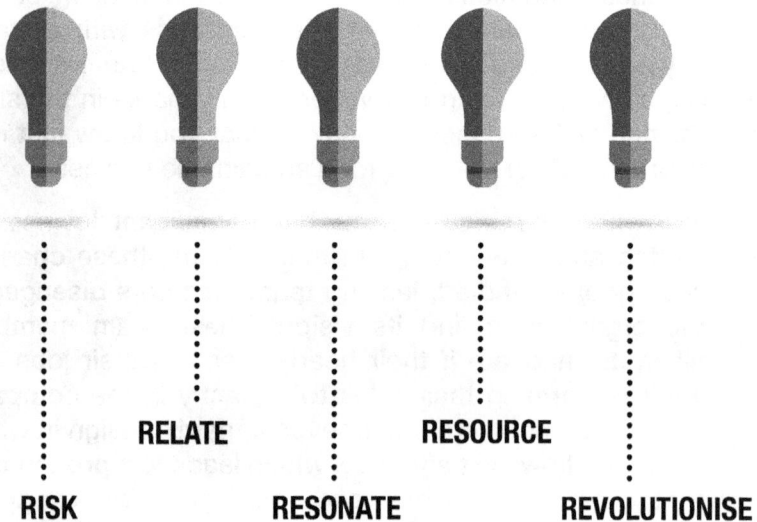

RELATE   RESOURCE

RISK   RESONATE   REVOLUTIONISE

you the tools and confidence to stare innovation down. Then, most importantly, work out how it can be integrated into your business.

While we will be discussing innovative practices, time will be spent at the junction where problem solving and engagement intersect (and sometimes collide). Building on the central themes of communication and trust, this book attempts to foster innovative and highly connected workplace cultures. The 5-step Innovation Accelerator method is uniquely designed to address the barriers you face and is supported by stories from several prominent CEOs, innovation award winners and ordinary leaders who are simply trying to make a difference. This method is for everyone – big budget or small. For every barrier, you'll find practical solutions, and, by combining all five of the steps, you'll be equipped to build an innovative culture.

Communication is the linchpin

Clear and authentic communication is the *sine qua non* of a connected, productive and satisfied workforce. It is also the innovative leader's superpower. This powerful force is always at your disposal. Effectively engaging your people at all levels is a critical component of the important Resonate milestone on your innovation journey.

I am going to repeat this strategic engagement theme in context at each step of the model, so if it looks like I am labouring the point, bear with me: it is for good reason. Communication is the backbone of engagement. Every positive interaction with an employee has the potential to spark a deeper engagement, which is a powerful innovation trigger. A workforce that feels informed and connected to the business direction will not only be more highly motivated, they will also get your brand closer to your customers.

The outcomes of the five steps are transformative. For instance, a former rival might start to look more like a worthy project partner, or you might find a new, unmined source of revenue. Whatever you hope to achieve, I hope this book gives you the impetus you need to boldly walk down the road to a more innovative, successful business. May it ignite your passion for innovation as the secret to sustainability and growth.

> Innovation is the impact you want to make, and it is achievable, provided the right conditions are in place. There is an intersection at which you engage with the needs of your customers and those of your staff. At this intersection you'll find the greatest potential for innovation.

ABOUT THE CEOS AND SENIOR LEADERS FEATURED IN THIS BOOK

I have been fortunate enough to work closely with executives who have taken chances and are beginning to dip their toes in the innovation pool. In some instances they are diving in headfirst! One thing all the business leaders who feature in this book share in common is the belief that innovation is continuing to play a major part in their success.

Dr. Keith McLean, Director of Manufacturing, CSIRO Manufacturing

Dr. McLean leads a team of 400 scientists and engineers developing solutions for high-tech Australian manufacturers. His team is particularly focused on research into biomedical manufacturing, chemical and fibre industries, metals manufacturing, and innovative manufacturing. CSIRO Manufacturing wants to grow new industries and create high value jobs while helping transition existing businesses into the digital age, where they can find new opportunities. Dr. McLean says he is driven by the desire to meet grand challenges, which is only possible through collaboration.

Dr. Elliot Duff, Acting Research Director, CSIRO

Dr. Duff led his team to patent a lightweight, handheld 3D laser-mapping device known as Zebedee. His team won the 2013 Australian Museum ANSTO Eureka Prize for Innovative Use of Technology. The system has already been used to map spaces that GPS cannot reach, including the Jenolan and Koonalda cave systems, Questacon, the Australian War Memorial, the Forum in The Hague, Fort Lytton, Peel Island, a WWI tank, crime scenes, mines, factories, remote forests and more.

Maxine Horne, CEO, Vita Group

Maxine opened her first mobile phone store on the Gold Coast in 1995. Today, Vita Group is Telstra's largest mobile phone retailer in Australia and an ASX-listed company. Maxine has used innovative strategies to turn her company into a highly successful group that operates in the retail, small-to-medium business and enterprise channels under brands including Telstra, Fone Zone, Sprout, Vita Enterprise Solutions and One Zero.

In her own words, "There's always a way – you just need to find it".

Paul McManus, Executive Director and Head of Global Enterprise Mobility, Telstra

Telstra has won recognition and awards for its innovation in the area of wireless 4G and 4GX networks, winning accolades at the World Mobile Conference in Barcelona for its Lanes technology. Introduced initially for the emergency services and the mining and resource sectors, Lanes (a dedicated mobile network service) enables Telstra to provide highly reliable and prioritised access to companies that operate in remote environments in which running physical cables or fibres is simply not practical. Paul's team continues to push through boundaries, and have the drive to innovate and evolve alongside disruptive technology evolutions.

Glen Babington, Executive Manager Infrastructure Services, Unitywater

Unitywater recently won an Australian Business Award for Innovation. The organisation is a statutory authority that supplies water and sewage services to the council areas of the Sunshine Coast and Moreton Bay in Queensland, Australia. Glen and his team are working to provide an innovative environment in which operations and the delivery of maintenance services are optimised. He believes that at the core of innovation is a culture of trust, inquisitiveness and respectful questioning of the status quo, none of which is possible without the explicit support and drive from the CEO and the board.

Scott Barnes, Manager of Mechanical and Electrical Services, Unitywater

Scott places a high value upon innovation, particularly when it comes to challenging the status quo. Doing so, he says, is the best way to see consistent improvements in business efficiencies. Scott's commitment to innovation made him an obvious fit for project leadership, and, in this role, he has been able to dramatically increase efficiencies – saving Unitywater more than half a million dollars each year.

Marcelo Bastos, Chief Operating Officer, MMG

Marcelo is a key member of MMG, a company founded in 2009 with the aim of building the world's most respected diversified base metals company. The organisation recognises the value of innovation to achieve growth and improve productivity. Supporting innovation across all aspects of the business has been key to Marcelo and his team's ability to deliver ongoing cost reductions and efficiency improvements even while mining and processing volumes have dramatically increased at most of MMG's sites around the world.

Geoff Wenborn, Former CIO, Origin Energy

Geoff is a senior IT executive with previous technology accountability in a number of major organisations. He was recently CIO at Origin Energy – Australia's largest energy retailer – with a diverse portfolio including electricity generation, natural gas exploration and production. Geoff is always on the lookout for the next industry-changing disruptive innovation.

Tom Potter, Founder, Eagle Boys

Tom built a multi-million-dollar pizza franchise business that became Australia and New Zealand's biggest privately owned business of its kind. Starting with one shop in Albury, New South Wales, Tom took the company to market leader with such innovations as the two-minute pizza. He was named the *Australian Financial Review*'s Young Business Person of the Year and was inducted into the Franchise Council of Australia's Inaugural Hall of Fame. Tom has since retired from his position.

Part 1:
The Innovation Show

CHAPTER 1:
Innovation: A Protean Term

Its rise to prominence over the last few decades means that 'innovation' is something of a protean term. It assumes a different form dependent on who is defining it. In essence, innovation involves something new from which you can extract value. This could mean introducing a new IT system or starting a new product line. It could involve turning an idea into a profitable commodity. It could mean leading your business in a direction that will enable it to better keep pace with competitors.

Innovation's scope is massive, and, though it's often linked with technological breakthroughs, there is much more to innovation than its association with technology suggests. In the corporate sphere, innovation has two pillars. The first pillar is dramatic and disruptive – like a tidal wave that washes a new way of living over the old. Innovations of this type seem to come from nowhere, changing the market, or even the world, overnight. This is also referred to as 'disruptive innovation', a term coined by Clayton Christensen to describe the process whereby customers gain access to a product or service that was historically only accessible to the elite (e.g., personal computers). Broader definitions include anything that, often in dramatic fashion, makes possible the overnight emergence of new markets.

The second pillar represents the culmination of years or even decades of small but noticeable improvements. Building on the concept of *Kaizen*, the Sino-Japanese word for 'improvement', this new way of looking at long-term corporate transformation reframes innovation from a sudden process into a continual one – one that seeks to build a better organisation, product or service through a cooperative effort that pervades the company's culture and processes. While it is the first pillar that most readily springs to mind when we discuss innovation, innovations of this type are few and far between. The second type encompasses a broader range of innovative practices: product improvements, new marketing strategies, incremental process enhancements, new ways of reducing costs or accessing customers – the possibilities are endless.

Myth busting

Build it and they will come

It is a common mistake to think that a great idea will, by virtue of its brilliance alone, gain traction. Every successful product needs a market, and the most noteworthy innovators tend to be those who are also best at predicting what the market needs – even if the market doesn't know it yet. Take Thomas Edison's first invention for instance: when the phonograph was first introduced, the public were spellbound. As something entirely unknown to potential customers, the phonograph disrupted the market by providing something that was as unexpected as it was desirable. Edison and his team had a hunch that the phonograph had massive practical commercial appeal. They tested the market to make sure they were on the right track and then introduced to an unwitting public a product that would make Edison a household name.

The brilliance of the invention is without doubt, but Edison didn't bring it to market until he was sure that it would be a commercial success. Patent offices are filled with the designs for brilliant products that have never made it much further than their first iteration simply because there is no clear commercial application for them.

Innovation is the work of a solo genius scientist or engineer

One person's success is never the whole story. Innovators don't operate in isolation. Edison had a mentor and a number of talented lab assistants and engineers. Edison and his team produced a number of failures before they brought anything successful to market. The same is true of innovative companies today: for every successful innovation, groups of talented people have undoubtedly made numerous fruitless attempts.

Edison built Menlo Park, an institution established with the specific purpose of technological research and production. Here, he systematised the process of invention, and it was this (as much as any of his inventions) that revolutionised the world of innovation and technology. He was perhaps the first to foster and model a culture of innovation. He was a strong leader, a powerful communicator, and he knew how to align teams with purpose. This was the key to his success. It was this model that kept him ahead of his competitors, and it remains a viable model to this day.

Edison also had a pioneering spirit, which never allowed him give up, in spite of failures. He epitomised the man who learned valuable lessons from failures. He famously said: "Fail your way to success", and this has since become the motto for many a leader to live by.

"We were the first people in Australia to sign up to SAP HANA (database management system) as an HP Services Model, but we tried to do too much with it too early on too large a scale. So, like all companies, there are failures and successes in how we implement some of those technologies and there are great learnings. Innovation requires a fast fail mindset."

– Geoff Wenborn, CIO, Origin Energy

Three types of innovators

Depending on timing and their market position, innovative businesses fall into one of three categories: the trailblazer, the fast follower, or the latecomer. Each presents its own opportunities.

The trailblazer

In this category we find innovation giants like Apple, Tesla, and Coca-Cola. The last of these has, without a doubt, been one of the world's greatest marketing success stories. Even with the tide turning against sugary drinks, their brand is as ubiquitous as ever. It is both the frequency and the volume of their communications with the marketplace that place them most firmly in the category of pioneering innovators. As the benchmark against which all other soft drink brands are measured, they own their product category. Though their competitors have attempted to challenge Coca-Cola's place atop the mountain, these attempts have, in aggregate, fallen flat. They have been unable to change the conversation, unable to redefine the market, unable to unseat Coca-Cola as the dominant market player.

The trailblazer knows that speed to market is important, but they also understand that having a high-quality and dependable product is the way to stay at the top of their category. Since their type of innovation introduces something often entirely new to the market, they may have the luxury of time on their side. This can enable them to perfect their product before introducing it, which makes it even more difficult for fast followers and latecomers to gain competitive traction.

The fast follower

The fast follower takes substantially fewer financial risks than the trailblazer. Since the fast follower innovates in the immediate wake of shifting markets, they can watch for and learn from the pioneer's mistakes. They may see opportunities that the trailblazer has overlooked. While it might not lead to product category ownership in the same way that trailblazing will, it will demonstrate a willingness to react quickly in response to the most recent market trends. Especially for smaller companies, letting others assume the often-substantial risk of pioneering is the best possible strategy (provided that when the market changes, they take action, so as not to be left behind).

"While being first to market is great, being the best in the market is even more critical. We went to market without trying to be all things to all people. We invested in innovation, and we had a plan: 1) Be number one or two in every market we are in; 2) Be the only pizza company in Australia that can supply pizza in two minutes. The implementation of the Two-Minute Menu was the way we would differentiate ourselves in the marketplace, because we knew customers wanted more than pizza; they wanted more time in their busy schedules. We found a way to give that back."

– Tom Potter, Founder, Eagle Boys

Speed to market, while not the first priority for the fast follower, is still important. The difference between the fast follower and the latecomer narrows considerably after a disruptive innovation has been introduced. In the digital age, markets mature remarkably quickly, so having structures in place that support rapid direction changes are absolutely crucial to prevent falling into the latecomer category.

The latecomer

The last of the three is the latecomer or late mover. This can include those who wait to innovate until the market has spoken extremely clearly about its direction and those who enter a mature market with a subtle (yet revolutionary) improvement on an existing idea. There is a hair's breadth separating the latecomer from the fast follower.

When in the position of deciding whether to be a follower or later mover, the most important criteria should be the product category's lifespan. If it is a new technology and the shelf life of the category is likely to be short, the advantage goes to the pioneer and the fast follower; their ability to get their product to market before their late-moving competition will see them capturing the lion's share of the profit in the short-lived market. If, however, the product category shows signs that it will be long lived, latecomers can bide their time and wait for the perfect moment to offer a product that improves on what the trailblazers and fast followers introduced at the beginning of the category's lifecycle. In age-resistant categories, it doesn't really matter who gets there first – it's all about producing a better solution while the category is still thriving.

This last point is worth repeating. It doesn't really matter who gets there first, so long as you figure out a way to produce a solution better suited to your customer's needs. You'll do this by establishing a workplace culture that encourages customer-centricity and rewards ideas.

In note form, this means:

- constantly innovating
- having a well-rounded management team
- valuing all types of talent, from sales and marketing to technical talent
- reacting quickly to disruptive technologies or business models
- don't be too proud to imitate
- don't be reluctant to walk away when it no longer makes sense to keep spending.

CHAPTER 2:
Buying Your Ticket to the Innovation Show

The red velvet curtain begins to rise slowly, the lights dim, and the crowd falls silent. You lean forward in your seat. In the middle of the stage, a spotlight reveals a smart pair of shiny shoes. The spotlight travels up to reveal smart corporate clothing, stopping on the wide smile of a successful, accomplished-looking leader. This person looks familiar to you.

Of course! It's one of your peers. To rapturous applause, she is demonstrating the latest app her company has brought to market. She has just won an industry award and she is revelling in the spoils of success.

Do you think you could be the one in the spotlight receiving awards (not to mention the applause)?

An organisation-wide focus on innovation is what will get you closer to the spotlight of success and the opportunities that will open up therein. We are all familiar with the charismatic leaders at the top of the world's most innovative organisations. They tend to have much in common; they tend, for instance, to manage the 'people side' of business extremely well. They ensure that engaging with their organisation translates to almost universally positive customer experiences, and this customer-centric business model is the driver behind their organisation's success.

The sooner you can purchase your ticket to the Innovation Show, the sooner you can dictate your relevance in your industry. Here's why:

1. We are all part of a competitive global marketplace; organisations that are the quickest to structure their organisations for flexibility, risk taking and collaboration are the ones outshining their peers.

2. If you stand still for too long to admire how far you have come, you will fall prey to the comfort trap; you'll miss the next innovation wave, and if your competitors take advantage of the emerging technologies that come with that wave, you'll be left in their wake. Innovation changes industries so quickly. It can reinvent overnight how the market perceives a product or a service, and, if your organisation isn't driving these changes, you will want, at the very least, to keep pace with them.

3. Corporate environments are ripe for fostering cultures of innovation. Once you start looking for it in people, processes and technology, you'll find it. The only questions are where you'll find it and how best to harness it.

4. To get close to your customers, it pays not only to understand their expectations but also to deliver on them more quickly than your competitors. Innovation is a powerful tool that will help you accelerate your speed to market. If you aren't getting to your customers fast enough, you can be sure that someone else is.

What keeps you up at night? Kodak's place in history

We could talk at length about what happens when people fail to innovate. The demise of Kodak—once a household name—is a case in point. It wasn't so long ago that they were the market leader in camera technology – affordable and accessible to all, their products earning them an enviable following. However, they were forced out of the market that they played a starring role in creating because they didn't heed the inevitable movement from film to digital photography. They made some attempts at film/digital hybrids, but hedged on making the vital pivot they required to keep abreast of market trends. This unwillingness to take the plunge meant that it was easier than it should have been for more nimble and innovative competitors to take their market share.

The moral of the story: Like the natural world, the world of business makes sudden (and often unexpected) evolutionary leaps. When a disruptive technology enters the market, you can adapt to the new conditions, or you can risk being pushed out of the market by a more agile competitor. The choice is yours – either stay with the pack or, like Kodak, become part of the fossil record.

Being innovative means being fearless

Fearlessness and innovation go hand in hand. Today's business leaders can't afford to back down from a challenge and, in fact, survival depends upon the ability to pivot in an instant, to innovate fearlessly.

However, there's no crystal ball to tell us when something is going to fizzle or become the next industry disrupting innovation, so it's important to combine market research with a certain amount of intuition. A strong instinct or gut feeling is something business leaders know all about. While intuition may not be tangible in itself, it is often premised on tangibles – market trends, forecasts, prior experiences with people and circumstances, etc. Let your intuition play a part in decision-making, but remember that it won't tell you things like whether a new product to the market is a game changer or simply a trend.

As your companion on this journey, I am here to guide you. This may mean making changes that are a little uncomfortable. However, the sooner you can embrace the 5-steps to innovation, the sooner you will see the rewards. Innovative organisations are those most likely to enjoy the following:

- Competitive edge
- Higher profits

- Greater market share
- Brand recognition
- Motivated staff that are easier to retain
- The ability to lure top industry talent

What it takes: Innovative leaders are more curious, clear and communicative at the same time. This is the blend of qualities you'll need to build better connectivity with your customers as well as your staff.

Teams will strap on their boots to take the innovation journey with you on the strength of this connectivity. A leader armed with integrity, an open heart and a solid plan will stand head and shoulders above the rest. Experience has taught me that if, as a leader, you demonstrate respect, communicate your vision and commit to the interests of your customers and staff, they will follow your lead without hesitation.

The innovative leader as trust-builder

Professionally and personally, your connections need to know that you know what you're doing. They need to recognise at a glance that you understand the niche you're filling, the trends within that niche, and how your employees and customers will be impacted. The 5-step Innovation Accelerator method, which we'll examine in more detail later, will guide you through the re-invention process. Not only will you and those within your organisation reap the rewards, you will also build the kind of trust and loyalty that market leaders enjoy. You'll do this by showing a readiness to innovate your way through or out of any sudden movements in the market.

Of course, it's not all about appearances. Authentic communication is key. Your leadership and ability to motivate your staff should elicit strong emotional responses from them. As the Kodak story illustrates, it pays to listen to those who have an eye on the market – especially when you know they have the best interests of your company at heart.

In order to take centre stage at the Innovation Show, building the trust of those around you is a great place to start. If you've let an opportunity pass you by, letting your competitors buy in ahead of you, remember that it may not be too late. Having built the trust of customers and employees alike, you'll soon be able to adapt to the new market conditions. Even if you didn't innovate ahead of the curve, the race doesn't always go to the swift. There have been many successes for organisations that are fast followers. We'll explore this in more detail in the next chapter.

CHAPTER 3:
The Price of the Ticket

I bumped into a client at a conference at which I had been speaking. A HR director, he was keen to introduce innovation, but said his company couldn't afford to invest in the necessary research and development. He was, he said, "flat out just keeping up with what we do now and managing the impacts of digital."

I get it. There are budget restrictions as well as knowledge gaps and talent gaps that make industry-leading innovation seem out of reach for organisations struggling to maintain market share. The ticket to the Innovation Show isn't free. It has a price tag attached. Budgeting for innovation, though, tends to lead to expanded future market share with the added benefit of customers feeling as though they are partnering with an organisation worthy of their business and respect.

"The invention of Zebedee was internally funded as a strategic project, which meant that it could fail without compromising on either the deliverables to a customer or our reputation. Having such internal money is critical to creativity."

– Dr. Elliot Duff, Acting Research Director, CSIRO

Sure, not everyone is fortunate enough to have a seven or eight figure research budget, but that's not necessarily the price of admission to the Innovation Show. Financing your innovation strategy will demand different approaches depending on the size of your organisation and your financing needs. Large organisations may have working capital available for investing in research and development and may be in a good position to borrow money from banks. For smaller firms and start-ups, banks may consider innovation a high-risk strategy, so this might mean exploring non-traditional methods such as angel investors, venture capital or even crowdfunding.

This book does not go in to the complexities and various methods of obtaining finance. The reality is that disruptive innovation (especially if it is a long-term innovation strategy) is going to cost money. Research, development, and market testing may mean sizable outlays. You may set out to achieve an objective and instead experience something different. There may be performance issues, or your product may need costly modifications before it is fit for purpose.

Ultimately, you need to work within your means and vision for the business. Weigh the costs of innovating against the costs of following your competition's lead: is it worth allocating budget to take a chance on a disruptive innovation? Perhaps getting the right specialists on board will enable you to focus on innovation in ways that will make your organisation more competitive? Each of these has a price tag attached, but the benefits can (and often do) far outweigh the initial costs.

If you've decided to start investing in innovation, there's good news: It is not all about a huge spend. There are many ways to be innovative, and you can start implementing them straight away.

Process improvement and problem solving

Innovation can be the result of encouraging and empowering your people to improve processes. For example, a client in a UK energy company brought me in following a large amount of change, to restore engagement levels and to put in place some systems for improvement. I led a series of problem-solving workshops with a mix of high and not-so-high performers to help them identify process improvements. The program ran very well, even though initially the client was concerned that only a handful of problems were properly solved.

Sometimes, it's not about the number of problems solved; it's about picking off the priority problems, and examining the problem-solving process itself. With the proper map in hand, there is a repeatable journey that can be taken — one that starts at clarity of issue and ends with a clearly defined solution. The workshops created a precedent for problem solving, not only for that group, but for the organisation as well. The real value was in the problem-solving method and its ability to revolutionise the way the organisation approached issues (both their own and their customers').

Crucially, the workshops also moved problem solving and process improvement up the corporate agenda, both formally and culturally. The time spent defining problems in the initial groups illuminated differences in perspective, requiring prioritisation and narrowing of focus. Frankly, reaching agreement on these aspects was half the battle. It also did wonders for morale as it helped the individuals take ownership of company issues and come up with solutions and outcomes within agreed-upon parameters that benefited not only them but their colleagues as well. Think of something as simple (but as important) as staff car parking or bicycle bays. Think corporate staff choosing to spend two hours per quarter to help out retail staff, walking the floors and asking customers what they would most like to see improved. Innovation is just as powerful when it is turned inwards to examine processes and problem-solving skills.

Innovative organisations are making money and saving money

Innovation is the cultural glue that binds you to your teams and to your customers. Therefore, creatively thinking about ways to solve your customers' and your staff's most pressing problems is directly linked to growth and profitability.

The world's most successful companies understand that innovation is the primary force that can drive market leadership and keep them one step ahead of their rivals. The trick is to navigate your people through bureaucracy and structures that tend to prevent or quash creative thinking. This might mean setting up cross-functional problem-solving teams or simply rewarding process improvement ideas. By solving customers' problems and rewarding staff for doing so you get a win-win. Creativity and problem solving should be applauded and rewarded, and where creativity seems to have hit a dead end, it might be up to you or design thinkers to step in and redefine the problem or provide other forms of guidance.

I mentioned that innovation doesn't have to cost a fortune. Sometimes even a relatively small investment can pay massive dividends. Unitywater, a company that has won awards for its innovative practices, has, through innovative partnerships and creative problem solving, managed to save millions of dollars that they were essentially flushing down the pipes each year. It was simply a matter of looking at the problem from a new angle – something that their innovation-first thinking made possible.

"We identified that there was a monopoly situation for the production and delivery of Magnesium Hydroxide Liquid (MHL) in the Australian market. We need MHL for reducing odour and corrosion in our sewerage network, so we partnered up with a local business to produce a comparable product. Once the product was refined, we built a batching plant on our premises, which the partnering company ran. Obviously, Unitywater had some large capital expenditure, but the business case and the internal rate of return just jumped off of the page. With the saving made, the MHL paid for itself within 11 months. We have ongoing savings in the realms of $600,000 per annum from our operating expenditure, and the more MHL we use, the more we increase our savings year on year."

– Scott Barnes,
Manager of Mechanical and Electrical Services, Unitywater

CHAPTER 4:
The DNA of Innovative Leadership

Innovative CEOs cannot operate in isolation. The executive leadership team needs to share the same vision, company ethics and spirit of innovation. One of the key strands I have identified in the DNA of innovative leadership is the desire to push through boundaries as an organisation, to combine forces and share ideas in powerful and game-changing ways. A business that fosters a culture of innovation and enjoys widespread buy-in will always be better than the sum of its parts.

For whatever reason, quite a few of the Innovative CEOs I have worked with have been engineers. This is certainly not to say that an engineering degree is a prerequisite for innovative leadership! What is a prerequisite, however, is a sense of ceaseless curiosity, which is also fundamental when it comes to inspiring innovation in others. This starts with sparking the curiosity of team members and, like so many other great leadership qualities, leading by example is the best way to ensure that the qualities you're looking for pervade the organisation. If you are curious about people, processes and technology, your employees will admire and emulate that curiosity.

Problem defining and problem solving

By seeking clearer definitions of problems before looking for solutions, leaders can set a clear example for those at every level in the organisation. Like curiosity, this approach to roadblocks and tackling them with clear and effective processes has viral potential – it can be taught and spread rapidly throughout your organisation. Articulating the issues at the heart of an impediment to progress may be difficult, but it's also entirely necessary if you want to build a reputation as an innovative leader (and, indeed, an innovative organisation as well). Remember, only well-defined problems are solvable.

> Hot Tip: Take the time to look outside of your industry for innovative solutions. Deconstructing the root problems and their solutions in other industries may be useful as a workshop with a view to looking at applications.

Communication

Ultimately, timely communication builds credibility, which in turn builds rapport. Regular and effective two-way communication with and between teams makes members of your workforce feel they are contributing – and therefore valuable. Your employees will also feel that those at the helm are steering the ship straight. It stops the rumour mill from spreading misinformation and sets a high standard for organisation-wide practices of open and clear communication.

When you detect authenticity in a communicator, it is palpable. I worked as an adviser to a CEO who, at the time, was leading his people through uncertain times in a highly regulated industry. He used the opportunity of a forum with his top 400 leaders to raise the issues the organisation was facing. This included the status quo of the industry and the company's position within it, the regulatory environment, shareholder expectations, company financials, performance and safety indicators. He finished off his presentation by spelling out what he would like the team to focus on and then stepped away from the podium, moving to the front of the stage to speak from the heart with his audience. This simple and passionate manner of address rallied the troops; his belief in the organisation and its members was, to say the least, infectious. Following his presentation, an audience member turned to me and said, "I would follow that man anywhere."

> Communicate as a group or as individuals, but always with an aim to generate buy-in for the business goals. Above all, there must be support for the CEO and the decisions made as a leadership group. A united front displays a consistent strategic vision—as important during times of change as it is during business as usual.

Innovative team DNA

The make-up of top team members is critical, not only to your organisation's success, but also to its ability to foster innovation at every level. It is the responsibility of your top team to observe shifts in the market and to raise them with a view to discussing how they can be practically integrated into your business strategy. Innovative teams tend to be varied ones as well. By mixing it up – departing from the status quo and creating cross-disciplinary leadership teams – fresh ideas and fresh approaches can be brought to old problems.

Businesses are calling on new forms of expertise, (e.g., productivity managers, IT infrastructure experts, customer analysts, social media consultants, etc.) and these new positions are adding substantial value to leadership teams. Resisting such trends too quickly and *in toto* is almost certain to lead to a business that is substantially out of step with the times and almost certainly out of step with its customers.

Let's take a closer look at some of the qualities Innovative CEOs look for when assembling a leadership team.

> "You need a good, strong, trustworthy team around you that have the same or similar value set. You have to have the confidence that when you sit with your team and go, 'X, Y, Z' that you know

you're going to get X, Y, Z and not A, B, C. You absolutely have to have that confidence, and if you haven't then you need to change it. It's impossible for you to be a good CEO today without a great team around you."

— Maxine Horne, CEO, Vita Group

Balance

Leaders should be balanced, able to focus on the present while also keeping an eye on the future (especially when it comes to innovation both within and without your organisation). High-performing top teams should be eager and effective communicators who are also skilled listeners. They will be consulting with a wide range of internal and external stakeholders who will help them stay informed. Balanced judgment will give them willingness to handle complexity and things going wrong, rather than being paralysed by them.

Autonomy

You may have experienced for yourself the futility in trying to tell staff members *how* they should do their jobs; better by far is the team member with whom you are able to move beyond the particulars to the broader objective or vision. Empowerment starts at the top and should have a knock-on effect down the ranks in a hierarchical organisation and across divisions in a matrix-style company.

Positivity

It's hardly a secret that a glass-half-full perspective tends to inspire and engage team members more effectively than pessimistic leadership. If you want those within your organisation to push through and eventually overcome obstacles, those who lead them must continually spur them on – but without any trace of the defeatism that can make further effort seem futile. Your leadership team needs to be looking for opportunities to encourage team members to use their creative talents and problem-solving skills. Positivity and humour (especially when in the midst of a setback) goes a long way when it comes to boosting organisation-wide morale and improving the vibe of a workplace.

Openness

We talked about communication above, and, just as those at the top need to become powerful communicators, so too business leaders need to be equipped to gather and share information. They need to be good listeners, highly approachable and tolerant. If your leaders can't communicate effectively, it is unreasonable to expect those reporting to them to raise important concerns, escalate problems or even seek advice when they need to. I believe being personable is an influential trait in any structure. Remember, engagement is a trust and loyalty game, facilitated by communication.

First-rate trouble-shooting skills

By virtue of being leaders, it is implied that your top team should act as ambassadors for the CEO's vision and steer their teams towards the attainment of goals. I coached a middle manager regarding his daily activities and helped him refocus his attention to delegating more of his work to his able team. This freed him up to spend more time looking for problems and asking whether there were better ways to tackle issues. Collaboration was born! Regular interactions with his staff and examination of business processes within his unit helped him to craft a more powerful innovation strategy than would have been possible otherwise. He also got some quick wins in terms of customer delivery through the team creation of more efficient processes.

Recognising and rewarding

Your top team is those you entrust to identify talent and cultivate the sort of behaviours that will bring about a culture of innovation. Long gone are the days of a regular pay cheque being enough to retain your best staff. A good salary may be enough to *attract* good staff, but today's best employees want the ability to perform and be rewarded for this performance. Failure to recognise and reward innovation will make it extremely difficult to retain the kind of talent you'll need to succeed. One energy company I worked with recognised and rewarded people for abiding by the values of the organisation. There were safety awards, performance awards, awards for almost everything. Nearly everybody was recognised and rewarded for a unique contribution of one kind or another. When recognition is given genuinely and justifiably, it makes effort feel more worthwhile.

Visibility

Leaders in senior company positions who think they can lead via email or from behind a desk in reality are simply not in touch. While what they are working on is, in their eyes, the highest business priority and therefore warrants their undivided attention, this self-imposed isolation will ultimately cost them the trust and loyalty of their team.

I am the first to proudly announce that I am an introvert, but this is no excuse for being invisible. If leaders find themselves taking refuge in their offices, it is time to step out from behind their workloads and be present. Every team needs a leader. As so often is the case, absent leaders are generally—albeit unofficially—replaced by somebody else. This might be a natural influencer or it might be just the best communicator in the group. By leaving a leadership vacuum, you allow the next influencer a seat at the head of the table, and this person may not share your vision or even your ability to steer the ship.

Every CEO or MD counts on their leadership team to be ambassadors of the broader vision. They are relied on to step up and translate the company's key messages so that they are meaningful to each and every employee. I've seen particularly visible CEOs drop into team meetings unannounced to check the relevance of key messaging and how connected these teams were with their team leaders' versions of the vision. This is a great way to ensure that the same vision is being translated at every level and that the leaders are on the same page.

Activity: Getting your leaders on the same page

Innovative top teams are eager to take on the responsibilities for generating and managing idea flow. Some of the below might serve as a starting point for reviewing performance or job descriptions. All leaders should be able to identify and report back on these points, which are designed to help create a tangible (and trackable) culture of innovation. They include:

- Identify and nurture Innovation Champions.
- Monitor and refresh the Innovation Champion pool.
- Manage the innovation process through the Innovation Accelerator (5-step method).
- Sponsor innovation projects.
- Facilitate approval where required.
- Decide when and how a project should stop.
- Work with middle managers and individuals to build greater innovation networks.
- Communicate at every opportunity.
- Ensure there is a robust innovation idea and project tracking system.

There are practical steps that can be taken to keep innovation front and centre and one of these is what I call the Top Team Treaty. This is essentially an issues management agreement, which can be particularly helpful at times when a united vision and consistent messaging is critical. Introduce the treaty as a standing 30-minute agenda item in your top team meetings and then periodically check progress and address any conflicting messages or incongruent behaviours. It may look like the below example, requiring all leadership team members to sign up to it.

The Top Team Treaty

1. As part of our weekly business meetings, we will raise two hot issues or problems involving people, process or technology. We will also raise two new, home-grown ideas sourced from our Innovation Champions and other team members.

2. We will understand the context of the issue or the idea and listen to each other's views and reach agreement on the company's position on each.

3. We will not leave the room until, as a group, we have consensus about our position in relation to these issues and ideas.

4. We will ensure these position statements are crafted into key messages, which will be signed off by the team before the end of the meeting. Leaving the room with agreement surrounding key messages will enable the top team to disseminate and discuss (immediately following or at an agreed time as appropriate) as an action of the meeting.

5. We will do our part to communicate these key messages in a timely and consistent manner.

Actions speak louder than words when it comes to getting problems and innovation on the company agenda. By ensuring the Top Team Treaty is on the agenda, you make it absolutely clear to your team that the well-being of your people and their place in innovation is something that must be prioritised.

Part 2:
Innovation Accelerator: The 5-step Model

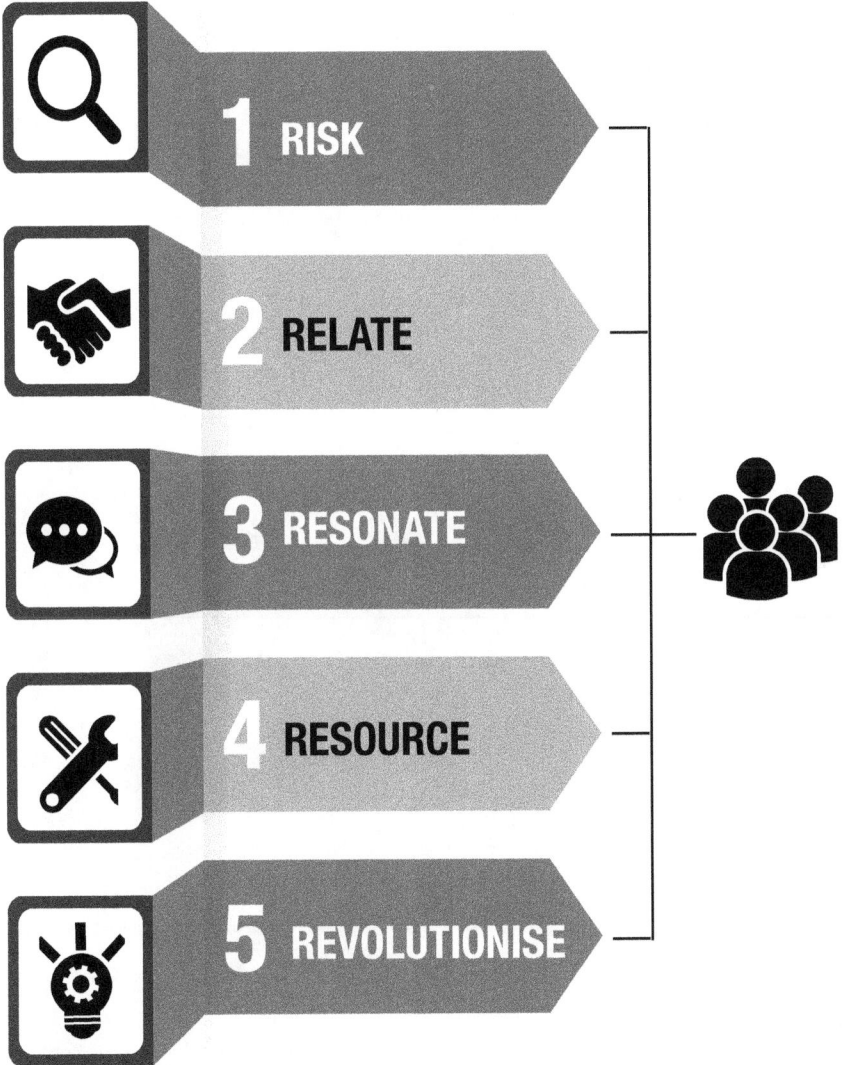

1 RISK

2 RELATE

3 RESONATE

4 RESOURCE

5 REVOLUTIONISE

INTRODUCING THE 5R'S

I have worked with leaders in many different industries (energy, mining, insurance, banks, media, retail, telecommunications, recruitment, and government) in Australia and in the UK. I have watched, listened, coached and helped leaders to discover creative ways to engage, using strong communication processes that keep information flowing – particularly during times of change. The bond of trust this has created has dramatically improved working environments, output and partnership opportunities.

Following years spent examining the cultures of different types of organisations, I have discovered a number of distinct patterns when it comes to how well they manage interactions between leaders and staff. In a tangible way, attitudes change for the better in the presence of practical guidance, a strong vision, autonomy, robust communications and change procedures. Not only this, but creativity flows more freely; people are inspired enough to lift their own performance, and innovation is given the room it needs to breathe.

The 5-step system that forms the backbone of this book is the result of my analysis of these patterns. The steps, in combination, form the foundation of an innovative company culture. Notably, I have placed staff and customers at the centre of the model. Every step in the method depends on a resilient and resonant relationship with the people in your company and the people your company serves.

In the next five chapters, we'll look at each of the five steps in turn.

Roadblock: No appetite for risk

At this roadblock, risk-averse board members may be reluctant to invest money or other company resources into something unproven or new. Alternatively, the leadership team themselves may be risk averse and this aversion may pervade the organisation.

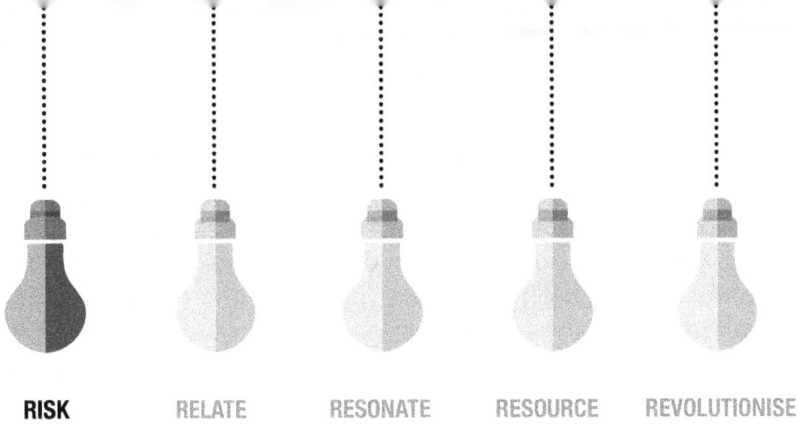

CHAPTER 5:
RISK

Solution: Create an appetite for risk

The unknown is not risk per se. It is only risky if you don't have a proven methodology by which you conduct innovation. Caution and reluctance are natural in the face of the unknown. This chapter outlines the strategies and RISK management activities that give boards confidence that innovation can be a repeatable activity resulting in big pay-offs or small losses with additional non-tangible benefits, such as learning more about your customers.

Gauging an organisation's risk appetite is a highly subjective exercise. Depending on whom you speak with, you'll get a very different assessment. Still, it's wise to look closely (and as objectively as possible) at your organisation and its attitude towards risk. Perhaps your management team is reluctant to take risks; perhaps it's your board; perhaps it's you.

CEOs (particularly in regulated industries) frequently come up against risk-averse boards. Indeed, requests for investment in unknown technologies can result in little more than raised eyebrows and polite refusals. It's not always immediately apparent how one should handle this. It's not sufficient to ask boards to simply "think more broadly".

At a conference at the Melbourne Business School, John Pollaers, Chairman of the Australian Advanced Manufacturing Council, noted a distinct lack of innovative thought patterns among Australian boards: "Our Boards have tended to focus on compliance and on efficiency gains – at the expense of new ideas. This means there is less focus on growth – in particular less focus on "intelligent growth" – and by this I mean growth through innovation."

Engagement is at the root of every aspect of this innovation journey and it is particularly prudent at the board level. The following items will facilitate strategic discussion:

- a set of key innovation principles
- enterprise-wide innovation strategy
- innovation plans.

Let's take a closer look at each of these.

Key innovation principles

Before preparing innovation strategies or plans as part of business as usual, a number of key innovation principles should be agreed with the board. These are essentially a few broad rules to help with innovation governance and on which the board can expect to approve or reject requests for support.

Examples of key innovation principles might include:

1. The idea/solution must help staff to attract customers: Proposed ideas/solutions will strengthen the relationship between the organisation and its customers. Agreement on such a principle might make it possible to explore entirely new ways to market, introduce external ideas, or even create a variation on a product that staff will be able to exploit in order to grab the attention of both new and existing customers.

2. The idea/solution must deliver (*insert objective here*) for the customer: defer to your company's vision or values statement as a guide to find the most appropriate

objective (e.g. the idea might deliver relief, cost savings, comfort, value for money or excitement).

3. The idea/solution must benefit the business model by (*insert outcome here*): If you want to improve specific areas of the business by introducing innovation, this is where you can nominate outcomes and reach agreement surrounding the criteria by which innovations will be measured.

These principles must capture the quintessence of the business strategy, reflecting precisely *what it is that you want your customers to feel/receive/do*. How an idea for innovation will tie in with the key principles will become fodder for internal communication, marketing and brand alignment – so it will become very useful. It keeps rationale for the strategic decision to explore an idea/outcome/solution close to your customer agenda.

Unless ideas meet the key innovation principles, they simply won't be acceptable; this helps keep the focus on what the company most wants to deliver.

Enterprise-wide innovation strategy

The enterprise-wide innovation strategy is an overarching, long-term document that dictates exactly how innovation fits in with the organisation's business model. The idea behind the principles and innovation strategy is that they will work in conjunction with existing governance frameworks and the business strategy. This enables specific innovation objectives, timeframes and measurements to be articulated. In preparing the macro innovation strategy it is fair to seek a clear indication of the risk appetites of the board members. This may be fairly apparent, but, rather than acting upon assumptions, agreement should be reached on the innovation maturity of your business and where it should be.

Innovation plans

Innovation plans are similar to business cases, in that a compelling argument should be presented which is supported by evidence. It is important to start from the problem you are planning to solve and define it well, then examine all aspects of the initiative. Each innovation plan must be factual, containing data on the people, processes and technology that must be made available in order to achieve each outcome or solution. The plan should contain budget estimates. It should list out resourcing requirements and impacts on existing staff. It should connect with the longer term innovation strategy and the business strategy. It should make a point of explaining how the desired innovation will help satisfy one or more of the key innovation principles. Agreement on tracking and reporting of progress should also be part of the innovation plan.

The perception of risk is lowered when decision makers have a robust innovation plan with the key innovation principles at its centre. The objective of the plan is to balance creativity with value creation for your customers. It's a common mistake to write business cases from our own perspectives rather than starting from the consumer insights that first produced the seeds of an idea. It pays to ensure that the plan accounts for the multiple stakeholders involved, both internally and externally. It should be very transparent, acknowledging real-world issues and risks.

The Revolutionise chapter goes in to the mechanics of piloting, trials and iteration in the context of innovation projects. However, you must start with an innovation plan which, while we know cannot define the outcome at the outset, will and should undoubtedly go through iterations of its own.

Innovative boards

Sometimes it's the board that wants to take risks, while the CEO and other senior executives are the cautious or reluctant ones. Take, for example, a mid-tiered company that has been running for 50 years. It has spent significant capital on equipment and developing people of a particular skill set. Governance and leadership structures as well as business practices have been in place for decades. When the board raises an idea for an innovation that will impact these structures, the notion of change or flex may be difficult for the executive team to rationalise or accept. In fact the leadership team might start to believe that the board is out of touch with the day-to-day running of the business.

This highlights one of the chief benefits of having clear agreement between the board and the CEO on the key innovation principles. It establishes a common ground on the topic of innovation for current and future discussions. Since innovative ideas are just as likely to come from board directors as they are from senior leadership, it's important to keep everyone in the innovation loop.

Third-party advisory committees are proving beneficial when it comes to providing expertise beyond that which board members can offer. These advisory groups monitor technology and innovation developments within or across industries, keeping senior leadership and boards informed of trends and helping them evaluate new ideas that might be a good fit for the company. Some companies, for example, are partnering with innovation or research organisations and using them in this advisory capacity. We'll discuss this further in the chapter on resourcing.

Innovation principles and enterprise-wide innovation strategies should be spurring everybody within the company to keep innovation on their radar. Every organisation has its more conservative members, and concerns need to be managed and doubts explored. Overarching innovation principles and strategies ensure that these issues don't slow down the innovation journey.

"My board requested that I, as CEO, do some serious thinking about risk and my ideas. Many of my ideas never got past a discussion or a paper – we had some really smart board people that would stop me from making fatal errors, so we would instead take quantified risks. When we rolled out the two-minute pizza concept, which was a huge risk, we took the concept and put it to a test market. We went into a market that was reasonably competitive otherwise, no matter what you did people would buy. So we trialled it in Newcastle (New South Wales) and ironed the bugs out and, once it worked, we rolled it out to the rest of the field."

– Tom Potter, Founder, Eagle Boys

Staff members failing with confidence

It takes a number of failures sometimes to get the outcome you are looking for. It also takes resources and ideas to keep battling. When things don't go according to plan or quite as expected, it is actually okay to communicate 'mistakes' or talk about trials that failed. This is all part of the innovation process, and this needs to become more than rhetoric. In some businesses, staff don't see the innovation vision as legitimate or urgent and, importantly, don't feel empowered to be forthcoming with ideas. This is where good communication is crucial and a transparent strategy and structure around the drive towards innovation will add a level of comfort.

I can recall an innovation engagement strategy that managed to demonstrate reinforcement of the company vision via the CEO publicly acknowledging the hard work of the team that had been responsible for the company's biggest failure in each quarter. While this was a light-hearted approach, it also strengthened the belief in learning from failure, and it later became an opportunity to reward success as an outcome of the earlier failures.

"For me, creating an innovation culture means everyone needs a licence to innovate, which means they need the licence to have a certain level of authority that enables them to fail but be forgiven

and try again. Modern reward systems need to underpin that approach."

– Geoff Wenborn, CIO, Origin Energy

Managing risk

It is beneficial to examine where the existing culture of the business needs to change so that new ideas can be more easily raised and accepted. As with any cultural change, you can expect that people are going to react. There may be strong resistance as emotional triggers like security or sameness are challenged. The innovation strategy must ensure the resisters and supporters are all accounted for.

Organisations such as government departments, bound by rules and legislation, can be more risk averse and can find the move towards innovation to be very challenging. This is particularly so when teams are used to following protocols and procedures.

Since innovation and risk are inseparable, here is a 10-point checklist to help you take calculated risks:

1. Know the daily activities of your customer (you'll need to do this to draft your key innovation principles).

2. Know your marketplace and competitors.

3. Seek agreement from the board surrounding key innovation principles, enterprise-wide innovation strategies, and innovation plans.

4. Interpret what this means from a change management perspective for staff.

5. Align innovation goals with key principles.

6. Use the wisdom of advisory boards.

7. Have your stage gates in place so you can regularly monitor progress and feasibility.

8. Support the supporters and empower your leaders.

9. Keep communication channels open at all times.

10. Know when to walk away if the idea is no longer a good one.

"The idea for the MHL (Magnesium Hydroxide Liquid) project got the support of my executive and then it went through what we call an asset steering committee, which is a governance committee that oversees the investment of capital funds. In terms of risk, because we are a monopoly and we are regulated, we have to prove that any expenditure that we make, especially in the capital space, is both prudent and efficient. So I produced a paper, presented it to the asset steering committee, and got endorsement, which meant that I got the required funds and also a project manager to assist in the build and so, got the green light for the go ahead of the project."

– Scott Barnes,
Manager of Mechanical and Electrical Services, Unitywater

Case Study: risk

Great example: Jim Donald, CEO, Extended Stay America

Why: Jim put an end to fears employees had about taking risks.

How: He transformed a culture that had been through negative change into one of fearless risk-taking and hope.

Details: Jim Donald took over a hotel chain that had suffered bankruptcy and, understandably, staff were quite wary of losing their jobs. This meant they were unable to think outside the square to improve the company's financial position. If, for example, customer service wasn't up to scratch, complimentary stays weren't offered to the dissatisfied customer. Staff were scared to act, worried that costing the company money might cost them their jobs.

In came Jim, who printed out 'Get Out of Jail Free' cards for each of his employees. This was his way of letting them know that they had his permission to take a risk on the company's behalf. What do you think happened? One emboldened staff member cold called a film production company that was coming to her city. The bold move brought the company $250,000 in accommodation bookings.

The moral: Jim took a calculated risk, which was enough to encourage not just this one individual but others to follow suit – a clear illustration that the first step to a culture of innovation is building the organisation's risk tolerance.

Roadblock: Innovation is a 'nice to have', not a 'must have'

A fundamental roadblock is the belief that innovation is optional. Underlying this is misplaced confidence that maintaining the status quo is sufficient to sustain business and customer interest. This manifests in reactivity to the market rather than proactivity and underestimating the power of staff in building a critical bridge with customers.

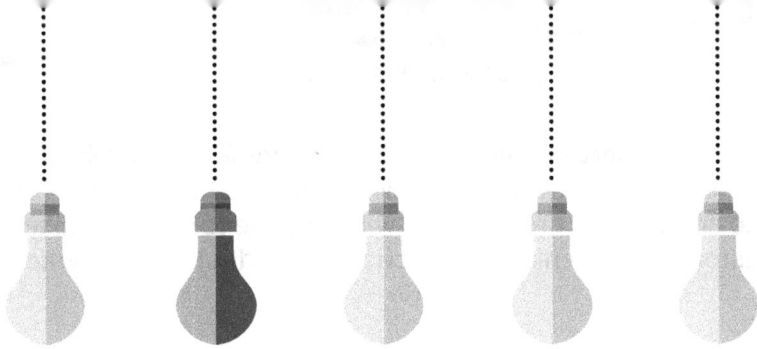

CHAPTER 6:
RELATE

Solution: A shift in mindset

Sometimes it takes a burning platform to inspire action. Here it is: Innovation is not optional. It is the key to the maintenance or improvement of your current market position.

The essence of RELATE is in creating a customer-centric culture. Ensuring your business is as close to your customers as possible equips you to react to the market. It means collaborating with trustworthy partners, engaging with customers, and making sure your business model is agile enough to move in response to shifting consumer behaviours and market trends. Whether it be your service offerings, products or processes, you need to be well informed enough to move with or ahead of the market. There's a good chance that your competitors are also more nimble than ever.

It begins with high quality information – finding out what your customer segments are thinking, feeling or doing every day. Meeting the needs of your customers ought to be the pulse of your organisation and this pulse needs to be checked daily for signs of change.

In a growing number of industries, speed to market is the difference between success and failure. Your ability to develop products and services that are new and immediately relevant to customers depends upon your willingness to innovate. This is how to ensure your organisation will continue to provide value for its customers – even in rapidly changing industries or markets.

Relating to the 21st-century customer

Do investments in innovation always pay off? No. Sometimes they will, however, and you can be guaranteed that *every* iteration, trial or pilot – successful or not – will result in a clearer picture of what your customer wants (or doesn't want). Technology is changing at a lightning pace, and so too are the customers using it.

We have established in earlier chapters that innovation is not a trend – that it can be seen in ancient civilisations as much as modern ones. People have been innovating for millennia. The difference between then and now is that the pace of innovation has quickened. Technological advances and the opportunities that the global marketplace presents to customers would have overwhelmed the ancient Etruscans. It would be fair to say that business as usual, as we know it, is no longer a safe bet for the future. This is particularly true for those in the resources industries, where still-rising demand is poised to outstrip supply in the foreseeable future. This is no time to get comfortable. Changes that can be glimpsed on the horizon will affect all companies large and small. Any beliefs that innovation is a nice to have, but not a must have, means missing out on the opportunity that innovation offers to get your business closer to your customer. That customer proximity will be important if you want to be able to follow them *as* they move, not *after* they move. Without a plan for the future that features innovation, it's only a matter of time before you're leaving profits that could be yours to your more agile competitors.

RELATE means adding value at every stage of customer engagement with your business. An occasional brainstorm with the top team to discuss buying trends really isn't going to cut it. You also can't leave it with the IT department to manage, and you can't outsource it. It's time to engage with and relate to the 21st-century customer, and this chapter will show you how.

> "In our sector, our customers are already tech savvy. So to a large degree, for Origin customers, we have to improve on the relationship we have with customers (not a traditional strength). We must deepen that relationship with our customers through both new and improved services that might be related. For example, managing energy needs in your home."
>
> – Geoff Wenborn, CIO, Origin Energy

Bridging the gap between staff and customers

The employee or staff base of a company tends to be the eyes and ears when it comes to knowing customers' wants and needs. They are also the face of your company. An employee who feels heard, supported and cared for will be more likely to provide customers with a similar degree of attention, support, and care.

This chapter is not about nurturing your employees, although it is an extremely valuable part of the method. It is, however, prudent that employees believe in the business and what it sells and are focused on helping to create a customer culture. The goal is that both customers and employees see in your products or services something that is highly desirable, timely, and appropriately priced.

Since more and more sales transactions are taking place online (where product-to-product comparison is a cinch), your employees have to be extremely well versed in the products they are selling in order to stay one step ahead of your well informed customers' questions and concerns. This reinforces the importance of ensuring your staff are well trained so that they are able to answer the kind of highly technical and complicated queries they'll encounter. For example, if a customer is dealing with a staff member who doesn't have the expertise to help solve a problem and the staff member neglects to put them in touch with someone who has the answer, the customer will be dissatisfied, and such an experience has viral social media potential. Knowing exactly what customers want is the currency of success. We'll return to this in the REVOLUTIONISE chapter.

> "The fundamentals of our business model have always been around delivering high levels of customer service to drive value into the sale. Our philosophy is: look after our people so they look after our customers, and the customers will keep coming back because of the environment we create in our stores and with our customers."
>
> — Maxine Horne, CEO, Vita Group

Disruptive innovations are a product of relating to customers

Disruptive innovation doesn't just create competitive advantage – it changes the landscape in an instant. When Steve Jobs launched the first-generation iPod in 2001, he solved the problems of access to a range of music, mobility and convenience – in one product. The companies that struggle the most in terms of frequent or semi-frequent market disruptions are those that sit on their hands at the most inopportune moment – namely, when a disruptive competitor has permanently changed the playing field.

Earlier, we talked about trailblazing versus fast-following innovators, and it's important to recognise that it is not just the pioneers that reap the rewards. Those who can follow on the heels of their disruptive competitors can often still beat their customers to market. They can even improve on their competitor's early offering. However, this means relating to customers before and during the disruption, listening carefully to their issues and, most importantly, recognising when and how a competitor has resolved these issues in a market-changing way.

Co-innovating or innovating with your customers in mind from the outset means you'll be able to offer them value-added solutions tailored to their *specific* needs. Netflix didn't reinvent the DVD, but they did recognise that the video rental/sale model was causing problems for their customers. By thinking about these issues and going to market with a solution, they, like Apple, solved a problem that many of their customers might not have been aware they had until the solution suddenly became available. This is the essence of disruptive innovation.

> "Origin is looking for what that next disruptive innovation might be. It is both a threat and an opportunity as we've got an established business model, so we could copy an innovation idea to break into a different market or disrupt our current value chain with the use of technology."
>
> – Geoff Wenborn, CIO, Origin Energy

High-quality customer information

Relating to customers in ways that will power innovation requires constant reinvention of ways to find data about them and their issues. This will inform your production of solutions that they will ultimately find appealing. Customer surveys can help. They can be as short or as long as you wish but be prepared that surveys will only reveal what a customer is prepared to divulge in that given moment.

If it's a nuanced understanding of your (actual and potential) customers that you're after—and it should be—big data is worth exploring. It provides access to customer information from databases, transaction records, mobile location data, call centres, digital pictures, and hits on websites, just to name a few. Big data can do more than improve your existing processes; it can also help you discover new market opportunities.

Here are four good reasons to invest in big data:

- Real-time data that depicts customers' shopping habits enables you to forecast and tailor products (e.g., Amazon can trace browsing behaviour on their website to suggest products that might appeal to customers based on their search and purchase history).

- You gain better knowledge of customer segments.

- It gives you the ability to match relevant offers with customers based on their locations.

- Linking data from online transactions gives the data holder precise information about customer preferences and behaviours.

Data mining is helping innovative companies keep pace with accelerating customer expectations. Mobile technologies and expectations of an easy online experience have already dramatically changed the way that customers interact with organisations, and it is likely that this will continue. Ultimately, your digital marketing and IT departments should be working hand in hand with communications and other key business functions to share customer information and help put it to work.

We know that social media has changed the way we consume and interact with brands. Thanks to its combination with mobile technology, almost all customer segments are connected like never before (in some cases, connectivity is almost constant). The most digitally savvy companies are building rapport with customers through simple, uncomplicated, and unobtrusive social media content. Gifts can also go a long way if you are looking to grow your database, but, as with all content, it's important to frame the offer in such a way that the customer doesn't feel as though they're being spammed.

We've already talked about technical advisory boards, which can prove extremely useful to businesses seeking insights and feedback surrounding technology trends. In the same way, customer advisory boards can provide invaluable advice around market issues and trends. Provided they have their fingers on the pulse of your target markets, they can provide fast insights, which can help you move quickly in response to even subtle changes in customer behaviours. This kind of insight can also help when it comes to product or service validation and acceptance.

The personal touch: the essence of relating

It's not new, but if you haven't done it for a while, engage your customers in conversation to ask them how you can further improve your service. Chances are you will hear something of value, and potentially from a different demographic than you would capture on your website, on social media or at events. In-person attention can be a humbling experience for a leader who has been removed from the front line – especially when asking people for their story and what it is about the product or service that made them select your company as a worthy supplier. Solidify the personal engagement by sharing something personal about yourself – you'll be surprised how well this resonates with customers. To make an impact, you only need to be personable, honest and strike the right note with a small handful of key messages. Not only is this great relationship-building the old-fashioned way, but word of mouth is still powerful, and you can bet that a positive connection established through open conversation will be replayed for your customers' friends and family. The feedback could also lead to a productive conversation with your product team or even make for a great blog post.

None of this is new, but it is more relevant than ever in an age in which face-to-face interactions are fewer and farther between. Customers are bombarded with information, so a pleasant and highly personal interaction feels more novel than it actually is.

"One of the things we've done from day one is be that local personalised presence. So, for example, we have events where we'll invite customers in to give feedback on what we're doing and talk about the latest and greatest products. We visit businesses and we have a CRM that collates all the relevant information. We take feedback from our customers very seriously. We do quite a bit on social media as well, and all of it is aimed at getting feedback so we can make sure that we're still relevant. The thing about being personalised is that it must be relevant to you."

— Maxine Horne, CEO, Vita Group

Customer culture creation

A customer-centric business is one in which there is an ongoing conversation. It's easy in larger organisations for employees to lose touch with how customers feel about the products and the organisation as well. In instances like this, staff members may forget what brings a customer to purchase in the first place (i.e., what creates the want or need).

Relating starts with empathy for customers and getting into the habit of thinking about their goals and buying habits. First, you have to understand what your customers really want; then you need to use that understanding when making product or service decisions.

Here are a few exercises to try with your teams:

1. Choose a customer segment and immerse your team in it. Adopt identities and go undercover. Personally ask real customers what they think about your products and what they think is missing. This is a great opportunity.

2. Go through the purchase cycle and examine each facet of the experience. Use your senses to determine what you like, don't like, see and feel. Think about what could improve the customer experience and make a list of at least three things that could be added to the experience to make it better. Then find at least three faults – even if they are minor. What sort of problems do people in your customer segment usually report? Use your organisation's customer channels and register a complaint that mimics one of your customers' most frequent issues and see how your employees respond (either positively or negatively)

to complaints. Repeat this process for each stage of the process from buying a product to returning it.

3. Discuss customer analytics and sales patterns at least on a weekly basis with your team members, whether they are customer facing or not. Big data is readily available, so discuss as a team some trends, case studies and stories focusing on both the good and the bad examples.

4. Identify the touchpoints in your business and who interacts the most with your customers. Reward those who consistently go the extra mile to help customers and those who bring back concrete suggestions for improving weaknesses in customer care areas.

5. Find out as much as possible about why competitors are getting your business. Ask your competitors' customers what distinguishes your organisation from the one they've chosen to do business with.

6. Ensure significant customer insights are shared widely as part of leadership communications through your company. What your customer is or isn't doing is good information for team meetings.

There are many techniques you could try to engage customers in your innovation process, from co-creation of brands and products to sharing their stories on social media. Increasingly, differentiation is more about the value your business can provide to your customers.

"We weren't going to go down the price competition route, so we decided to differentiate ourselves based on customer service. We have a program called CARE (Customers Are Really Everything). At first, it was the little things: back in the early days when you bought a new phone, you had to buy it, charge it up, let the charge come down for 24 hours and then recharge it, so we started doing that for our customers. We had Kids' Zones, where kids could be occupied with toys, pencils and books, whilst we were talking to the parents about the phones. We had coffee vouchers for nearby coffee shops, which we'd offer to customers whenever we were busy. We've kept finding new and better ways to provide that little bit extra to our customers."

— Maxine Horne, CEO, Vita Group

"We really want to help our customers and, increasingly, we're trying to embed people in our customers' business and have our customers embedded in CSIRO so that we can truly and more broadly understand our customers. It's a different approach to saying, 'Let's just make a widget that goes bang'."

— Dr. Keith McLean, Director of Manufacturing, CSIRO

Case Study: Relate

Great example: Bob Farrell, former entrepreneur and motivational speaker

Why: While he passed in 2015, his philosophy for business success (take care of the customer) lives on. His "Give 'em the pickle" principle is as relevant today as it was 50 years ago.

How: Farrell worked in retail before becoming a franchise pioneer of Farrell's Ice Cream Parlours, opening 130 stores and eventually selling them to Marriott.

Details: At Farrell's first restaurant, he received a letter from a disappointed customer who claimed to have been going there for hamburgers twice a week for three years running. The customer asked a service staff member for an extra pickle and was told that the side of pickles would cost her $1.25. The customer said she only wanted one extra slice and that the other staff members would usually give it to her. The staff member refused to budge. As a result, the customer wrote a complaint letter to Farrell, who personally apologised, reassuring her that it wasn't the way they run their business and asked the customer to come back.

As a leader, you need to make sure that your employees are permitted and expected to give 'em the pickle, no matter what your company's 'pickle' might be.

Depending on your business, this could mean:

- giving a customer a free month of service
- offering a refund if something goes wrong
- surprising a loyal customer with a free gift.

The moral: Go the extra mile to make customers happy and put your own personal stamp on it. A bit of old fashioned customer service is exactly what connects customers with brands at a time when loyalty can be lost in an instant.

Roadblock: Our business has a lot of people problems and they are change fatigued

Since the GFC, most companies have been through some kind of restructuring, downsizing, regular IT changes or a combination of these. Symptoms may be low staff morale, low productivity levels, overwhelm, disengagement, or disconnects with middle managers. These cultural realities represent a reluctance or unwillingness to innovate.

RISK RELATE **RESONATE** RESOURCE REVOLUTIONISE

CHAPTER 7:
RESONATE

Solution: Rally the troops

We have all heard of workplaces where relentless pressure combined with constant change has pushed employees to (and beyond) their limits. Whether these problems began under recent leadership or are inherited, there is a brighter and more stable work culture that can be created, given the right tools and leadership. This chapter focuses on overcoming the past, acknowledging the changing present, and putting in place a culture of innovation for the future. We'll be making use of two more important R's here: repair and resilience. Before we do that, though, let's start at the beginning with corporate values.

The company value proposition

Why are staff attracted to some companies over others? Pay and conditions certainly play a big part in this, but so too does shared values. Values statements support the business brand and are usually highly visible, obvious to employees and customers alike. They are designed to be ambitious yet attainable, essentially letting everyone know:

- the kind of personnel the company is seeking and will work to retain

- what is expected of staff (attitudes and behaviours)

- how customers are to be treated (i.e., what the organisation delivers and how it delivers it).

Representing much more than a bunch of words dreamed up by an ad agency, values are a key part of the brand of a business. They state in no uncertain terms how the company is intended to be run and how team members are expected to contribute. The point is there should be a commonality of beliefs in the company value system.

If these values have lost their impact or no longer represent the direction of the company, it's time for a refresh. This is a subject dear to my heart as a communicator: if you don't articulate and reinforce your current values and expectations, how can you expect them to be realised?

In the same way that you want your customer experience to be a uniformly good one, you also want your employees to be motivated and happy. This is not only about being altruistic. Today's culture-sensitive customers are attracted to organisations that have (or at least seem to have) a high-quality people culture that embraces customers and employees alike. As a business leader, you embody your organisation's brand and culture, so the buck stops with you if the brand is flagging or the culture is toxic.

If you are on the mission to attract and retain your industry's most talented people, the first step has to be articulating and promoting the employee value proposition. Since companies have a lot of values in common (e.g., safety first, personal and customer integrity, listen to our customers, etc.) it is important that you ask yourself exactly what reasons your workforce has to stay with your business. What's in it for them? Asking this question is all the more important when you are in the midst of transitioning to a model focused on innovation. Winning hearts and minds means being able to tie key messages to these very values as a rationale for the decision to invest in innovation.

When crafting or revising visions, values and mission statements, it's good to be ambitious. Take Coca-Cola for instance: their mission statement reads more like a revolutionary manifesto than a corporate document. Their stated mission is "to refresh the world" and "to inspire moments of optimism and happiness". They also speak of their leadership's responsibility to "shape a better future", of teamwork that "leverage[s] collective genius". There is also the usual focus on accountability, passion, and responsiveness, but these pale in comparison to the goals and expectations that they have set for themselves as an organisation. And what is the result? We see them doing exactly what they set out to do, attracting talent who are prepared to commit to these values and reinforcing their brand's ambitious vision in every market they serve.

The invisible contract between employer and employee

Something that can be overlooked in our busy work lives is the unspoken agreement between employers and employees: an expectation of mutual respect. If workers are expected to adhere to and embody the values of an organisation, they want to feel as though their contribution is valued and that they will not be overburdened with tasks or undercompensated for their efforts.

In a typical office environment, there is a plethora of technology to contend with. It may be no different in type to the technology channels you have at home, but there are certainly expectations attached to their use. Employees are expected to respond quickly to customers via email, keep up to date with industry and company news via intranet and Internet sites, and use mobile phones, desk phones and conference calls appropriately. Then there are competitor channels to monitor.

For example, staff stress levels might be high on something as simple as an IT upgrade purely because it is the latest in a line of changes. It's only natural for employees to sometimes feel overwhelmed and "over-communicated with". Overexposure of this kind can make even the thought of face-to-face meetings an added (and unwanted) pressure. Yet regular face-to-face meetings are absolutely critical in time-pressured environments, giving management the opportunity to 'health check' progress, and engage in mutually respectful dialogue that ensures staff know why their participation is needed.

Add this to the increased workloads and pressure that employees, middle managers and even senior leaders have been under since the GFC. According to a recent Deloitte report on the 21st century workforce, nearly two thirds of today's employees feel "overwhelmed" by the stresses of the job.

Streamlined operations have meant fewer hands on deck, and this means that, at every company level, people are putting in extra hours and enjoying less downtime. Such pressures in addition to constant change – organisational, structural and technological – impacts in untold ways your most valuable asset: your people. Understanding this is absolutely crucial in order to resonate with your teams.

> You can't create a culture of autonomous future leaders if you don't first empower them.

A little 'R' for resilience: the change to innovation spectrum

It is fair to question the wisdom of attempting to grow a culture of innovation in a company where changes (big or small) have been habitually resisted by employees. Culture is powerful and can just as easily break as make either planned changes or spontaneous ideas. Human nature is instinctively heightened by threats to the status quo, resulting in resistance – and this resistance can manifest itself in all sorts of undesirable behaviours. Have you seen staff reject a new IT system or not support a new initiative?

Innovation always requires change, so in order for your workforce to begin supporting rather than resisting it, they need to become comfortable with both 'the new' and 'the unknown'. This in itself may prove to be a transition; the culture of your organisation must become resilient. A resilient organisation is one pervaded with adaptable, flexible operators who understand the importance and benefits of change – whether planned or reactive.

> "One of the reasons why I think innovation is getting traction in our business is that it is being very much led by the top from

> the top. We've got a CEO whose motto is "always respectfully question the status quo". This has built a culture in which lateral thinking is actively encouraged. If you don't have that view at the top, it's very hard to get innovation going."
>
> – Glen Babington,
> Executive Manager Infrastructure Service, Unitywater

I have found that moving people along the innovation spectrum requires first addressing the history of change management in the business (i.e., processes that transition people from a current state to a defined future state with an eye to minimising impacts on the individuals and teams involved). Change management ensures that those who are part of a change process are informed, participating, and trained as required.

Managing impacts, adoption, embedding, etc. are too often the last considerations for those on projects. This can translate to the creation of a culture where people impacts are more of an afterthought. It's far better to start early and jump out ahead of any people issues before they arise. Change management is not just necessary when an organisation is in the midst of large-scale changes. Smaller changes that may be as simple as a technical upgrade may appear to have little impact on your workforce, but when analysis is done on the current versus the future state and role changes, for example, there could be significant skills gaps or other pending disruptions.

Prior to implementing a new system or a new structure, there are a number of steps that should be taken. These include impact assessments, change management activities such as communication, sponsorship, training, leadership coaching and resistance management. Planning for resistance is just as important as the other change activities. Managers need to feel confident that they know what they might be up against and when it is appropriate to intervene. This is where knowledge of workforce history becomes valuable.

The underlying reasons for resistance

Post GFC, workforces have faced significant changes through downsizing, redundancies, restructuring, amalgamations, acquisitions and closures of unprofitable divisions. In your organisation, such changes may have occurred; they probably made fiscal sense, and the company may actually be in a better position than it was pre GFC. No matter what the reasons that made structural transformations necessary in an organisation, it's important to recognise that periods of change and uncertainty have often-serious repercussions on the psyches of those who are still at their desks when the smoke clears. Such negative experiences can have long-lasting ramifications, making people resistant to further change.

When exploring the reasons why employees are resistant or reticent to do things differently, look for symptoms of overwhelm, disengagement or apathy. Alternatively, there may be vocal opponents of ideas or improvements of any kind. Have you noticed an increase in days lost to illness or extended leave? Has it come back to you that some of your employees are actively applying for jobs with other companies?

The rate of change is so fast that neglecting to put the appropriate change management processes in place is an easy mistake. However, it is a short-sighted and lethal one. When pending change will affect the way a group of staff perform their jobs and they are left out of the engagement loop, there is likely to be a big price to pay. Like a particularly nasty flu bug, this kind of discontent can become highly contagious.

Suffice to say, poorly handled change will not inspire positive staff outcomes and is likely to result in poor adoption of anything new. It certainly won't boost performance or inspire the kind of lateral thinking you need for the creation of a culture of innovation.

The maths:

Planned change
+
Change management

= Smooth adoption + Staff feel respected

Staff feel respected
+
Freedom to innovate

= Motivated + Productive workforce
(essentially, the beginnings of a culture of innovation)

Another good 'R' – repairing the culture

In the situations described above, where there is an individual or core group of resisters who, for one reason or another, cannot bring themselves to approve of new ideas or participate in collaboration, it is possible that these employees have, in their minds, been at the receiving end of profound injustices. For example, they may have been deeply affected by seeing their teams change around them, or their colleagues lose their jobs, and, as observers they've felt wounded, ignored and powerless. Sometimes small structural changes can have a big impact on long serving employees.

This is where cultural repair is absolutely necessary to reconnect employees with the organisation and its leaders. To do this, though, the issues that have caused resentment, resistance and negativity need to be brought to the surface. Only then can these bridges be mended.

It is a mistake to leave disillusioned staff to their own devices, in the belief that over time they will re-align themselves with the company vision. The reality is that they probably will not. This is where the opportunity presents itself to turn this situation around, acknowledging their pain and turning the experience into something positive.

These very people can become your closest allies, provided you take the opportunity to restore trust. In particular, those most passionate resisters, if listened to and empowered to be part of a new process or vision, can become your biggest champions and may have a considerable influence on the views of their colleagues. The truth is that they have probably longed for the right person to hear them and because they haven't, they have felt disrespected. Giving your attention and taking the time to listen as well as making earnest attempts to steer a fresh course means providing them with the consideration they may have felt they deserved all along. They must now feel enabled to make valuable contributions to the new direction; and they must feel empowered to help assess what lessons of old could be taken into the new world.

Great leaders are individuals who will take time before implementing ideas, not to hedge, but to identify resisters and tackle areas of low engagement. The onus will be on you and your team to repair situations when it becomes clear that adequate time has not been spent communicating and embedding change in the past. Ultimately, it means frank conversations need to take place between line managers and the staff members involved. The longer you wait, the more difficult these conversations will become.

When there is disengagement, confusion, or resistance, it is up to leaders to act and speak with courage and confidence. This means admitting where things could have been better handled or could be improved. Then the next step is to commit to appropriate corrective actions, and keeping affected people in the loop. If it's trust that you need to establish between you and your staff, follow through on these commitments. When you're repairing the culture, the newfound trust you're building is fragile. Be true to your word and you'll not only help manage change, you'll also inspire your people to help build and participate in a culture of innovation.

Positive leadership: leading change

Almost all of the CEOs I have worked with have had positive dispositions. As inspirational leaders, they encourage their employees to be the best they can be, which starts with taking a genuine interest in their aspirations, both personal and professional. They show resilience when they encounter unforseen issues, and they celebrate and reward effort.

> "Optimism is an essential ingredient of innovation. How else can the individual welcome change over security, adventure over staying in safe places?"
>
> – Robert Noyce,
> Co-founder and co-inventor of the integrated circuit, Intel

Employees can feel exposed when it comes to participating in innovation, which often demands that they leave the security of what they know to having to share their ideas (exposing them to criticism). Deliberately building or rebuilding trust through positive and authentic communication is a critical part of setting the scene for a more innovative workplace. Trust is only possible when employees feel empowered, informed and respected. You can future-proof change initiatives and avoid negative fallout by following the change management checklist provided below. Remember, this change checklist should help you pre-empt any enterprise-wide IT upgrades, software introductions, or other changes that will affect the way people perform their jobs:

1. Understand and sponsor the change.

2. Brief your change/communications manager and agree on a change and communications plan.

3. All change requires careful communication. This means key messages must be agreed by the senior leadership team when the decision is made to proceed with the change.

4. If you have Change Champions in your business, brief them on the initiatives first, gauge their reactions and get buy-in prior to alerting the rest of the business. These Change Champions may also help test a solution if it is an IT change and can step into that phase of the project.

5. Consistency and genuine belief in the change must be visible in the leadership team. If it is an unknown entity that is being trialled, be honest and call it a trial. Also, there needs to be organisation-wide clarity as to the expected outcomes of the change.

6. Ensure that the proposed change provides opportunities for staff to buy in, to upskill, and to be kept in the loop.

7. Ensure that, prior to implementation, employees have had discussions with their line manager and are completely comfortable with how changes will impact their particular role and the roles of those around them.

8. Identify change-resistant pockets or individuals prior to implementation. These also might come to light during testing (provided there is a change manager working with the team leader to monitor the feedback). Some degree of resistance can be helpful (highlighting, for instance,

flaws in the implementation method or the technology/ process itself).

Resisters might challenge the merits of a particular product/ process. While healthy criticism should be encouraged, adamant resistance or negativity campaigns should not. Separate conversations will be required with those who strongly oppose the company's new direction and they will need to nominate whether or not they are prepared to be part of the solution.

If employees aren't in the right headspace for innovation, it's possible that there are legitimate barriers that should be examined. Innovation comes in all shapes and sizes, and I fundamentally believe that, provided the conditions are right, there is an innovator in everyone.

Aligning teams with purpose

Transforming your organisation into an innovative one will take more than hard work from your people. They will also need to think laterally and extend themselves beyond their own roles. This means rallying your team around achieving goals, and delivering a timely and innovative result, or it might mean stopping 'busy work' in favour of an agreed set of priorities. Clear and open communication of these priorities lets those involved in the process know exactly where they stand, why the initiative is going ahead and when.

A focus on innovation can revolutionise the way your teams work together. It can promote peer collaboration, break down silos, and provide new ways to stimulate (and reward) idea generation. It's noticeable in organisations powered by innovation that employees feel safe enough to raise what they perceive to be improvements or solutions to problems, whether people, process or technology related. Innovation-focused organisations ideate or improve at every level of the organisation – they don't cordon off discrete areas in which particularly bright individuals are expected to produce results in isolation. No, it is the responsibility of all staff to bring all their potential to bear on the organisation's future; it is everybody's responsibility to participate in the sharing and evaluating of ideas. Each member of the organisation should be exploring customer needs so that the organisation can be one step ahead of these needs.

> "We have an innovation team as part of our Chief Technology Office which is full of technologists and engineers working on the latest technology solutions for our customers. But beyond that, we encourage every staff member, in whatever role they have, to take responsibility for innovation."
>
> **– Paul McManus,**
> **Executive Director and Head of Global Enterprise Mobility, Telstra**

> "In this organisation, a lot of the really great ideas have come from people at stores or people that, for example, sit in a Learning and Development team, where they keep getting the same issue raised with them all the time, and they say, 'Well, why don't we address this?'"
>
> **– Maxine Horne, CEO, Vita Group**

Due to the nature of constant change in our lives, we all look to position and frame – to group, categorise and label in order to simplify. In the absence of simplification and direction, assumptions are made. How this translates to your staff is that they may be prioritising and producing output according to what they think you want, or what they think is best. To avoid this, every opportunity needs to be taken to align teams with purpose. Ensure their efforts to better their circumstances or those of the customer are worthwhile. This way, staff initiatives are more likely to be on track with the company vision and time spent on development and testing can be justified.

Putting your people in the picture is essential to being able to sell a vision. Your staff will want to understand what it means to them. Until they understand the *rationale*, they are unlikely to think about *how* they can meet expectations. Be especially clear about the benefits (for your employees but also for your customers) of the initiative and how these benefits tie in to the strategic direction. This kind of context makes a more compelling argument for change.

Change Champions

The thought of acquiring new skills or knowledge can make even high-performing employees a little nervous. This is where Change Champions come in. In every change program it is wise to seek out the influencers – whether they be in the senior ranks, on the shop floor, at the security desk, or in the cafeteria. In every organisation there's a pecking order, and the best influencers aren't always neatly aligned with corporate structures. It's extremely helpful to make allies of these influencers. Their reputation as the strongest, most vocal, longest-standing, or wisest members of the organisation will go a long way when it comes time to get the rest of the organisation on board.

Influencers have one thing in common: they are passionate about the organisation and its members. This passion is the key to their influence, and, so long as you are able to convince this influencer that the proposed innovation is in the best interest of the organisation and its employees, they can be relied upon to bring others into the fold. Given the right support, they will be the sort of people you can rely on to get behind an initiative and to act as the eyes and ears for you and your employees alike. They act as two-way information channels, so just as they can keep you updated on how a certain innovation is being received, they can also keep their peers up to date on what you're doing to handle any staff issues. Perhaps most importantly, they can disrupt the rumour mill, providing much-needed clarity where there would otherwise be assumptions and confusion.

Bringing your Change Champions into the fold prior to a change will help you spot any problem areas or issues that are likely to arise. It is always better to identify the resisters, but build momentum with your influencers. To be most effective, your Change Champions need to feel like more—much more—than points of contact or informants. You'll want to make them feel respected for the important role they are playing in the organisation's progress. This will mean a highly personal mode of engagement, one that shows that you have an unselfish interest in their role within the organisation and their job satisfaction. Inspire them and then harness their energy to keep the momentum going.

Innovation Champions

Your Change Champions and your Innovation Champions may be one and the same; however, their roles in establishing an organisation-wide resonance are very different. Innovation Champions almost always have an entrepreneurial mindset. They have distinct ideas about how to improve and create, and they feel that they have permission to go above their job descriptions to provide unique value to their organisation. They take risks in order to solve problems.

How do you spot them?

Innovation Champions are:

- imaginative
- autonomous
- persistent
- lateral thinkers.

Not only do they enjoy finding solutions to problems, they are highly productive as well, often going above and beyond to push their ideas through to fruition. However, this does not always mean that they are adept at navigating politics or organisational structures, and this can hinder their progress. Though they have expertise and are credible, they may lack the confidence needed to gather widespread buy-in for their own ideas. That is where senior leaders step in, providing the advice and support necessary to gain traction.

Innovation Champions often take risks within the boundaries of their role. Expand that role (giving them more autonomy) and you'll be granting them the freedom they need to explore different ways to analyse trends or to solve organisational or customer issues. Promote them if possible, but always into roles that will give their innovative spirit plenty of raw materials to work with. I have found that team leaders do well to make a point of taking the time to recognise and reward such enthusiasm and drive.

In a manner of speaking, fresh ideas are currency and businesses need to start trading. Generating money-making ideas from within organisations and embedding cultures of innovation is the way of the future, positioning these businesses for longevity. The more of your time and recognition that you can give to your Innovation Champions, the more valuable an asset they will become for you and for your business.

The magnetism of innovative workplaces

When employees are empowered and autonomous, they feel trusted. People want the opportunity to shine, and if you have a culture that encourages lateral thinking by rewarding big and little innovations at every level from the team to the individual, your organisation will become one that attracts and retains innovative employees. Attractive compensation packages pale beside a workplace in which innovative employees are rewarded and championed for their efforts and ideas rather than stymied at every turn.

In cultures founded on communication, appreciation and openness to new ideas, loyalty can spread like wildfire. Does mutual respect and trust between employers and employees sound familiar to you? It makes for a very appealing workplace, especially when coupled with the chance to do challenging and meaningful work. Most employees will confess that it is a powerful motivator to be given the chance to make a difference in the lives of others, producing tangible benefits. The point is made that your people need a compelling reason to be at work.

"One of the reasons people work is purpose: they want to achieve something. Another is mastery: we spend our lives wanting to get better at things. The third is autonomy: we're smart people and we want to be trusted and appreciated for being so. And so, for

> me, it is about creating this environment where we give you skills, we help you to become masters in other things other than what you were, and then we create an environment that allows you to demonstrate those new skills that you've learnt."

> — Maxine Horne, CEO, Vita Group

What actually motivates employees might surprise you. Here's a list of some of the more common motivators I encounter when asking employees what they find most attractive about the organisation they work for (or would like to work for):

- a great brand
- positive team culture
- clarity around what meeting and exceeding expectations looks like
- career discussions about goals (career management)
- on-the-job training
- ownership
- opportunities to contribute across functions (e.g. multi-department projects)
- flexible working hours
- inspired and inspiring co-workers
- commensurate rewards
- recognition and gratitude for efforts (trying as well as achieving).

The power of the last point above, gratitude, is easy to forget and greatly underestimated, particularly in large companies. Remember to show gratitude for the value that your employees bring to the table as individuals. If you hired them, think back to what it was you saw in them in the first place and re-connect. Sincere gratitude is one of the most powerful forms of engagement available to management.

It's not just about humanity, caring and the bigger picture. It makes good business sense. Take Google for instance: they've rapidly become one of the world's most desirable workplaces, and, though their compensation packages are generous, it's more about the culture of innovation that they have created and continue to build upon. Since they understand that employee well-being is tied to productivity and innovation, they offer a bevy of perks, including free food, massages, flexible work schedules, and trips to places like Vegas and Hawaii. Google also has a policy they call Innovation Time Off: Google engineers are encouraged to spend 20 per cent of their work time on projects that interest them, even if these projects aren't in the department in which they work. Gmail, Google News, Orkut, and AdSense originated from these independent endeavours.

This isn't new. What do you think Thomas Edison did for his staff? His employees were paid bonuses out of the profits on inventions, and Edison socialised with his staff, providing snacks and cigars, as well as telling tales, dancing, and even singing. Edison's offices contained an electric toy railroad that employees could play with, and there was even, for some time, a pet bear. Admittedly, a pet bear would probably not fly with today's workplace safety regulators, but you get the point: if you're trying to encourage innovation, injecting an element of fun into a work culture and making it the kind of place that people want to be can have a massive payoff.

Failure is not a dirty word

It has been ingrained in so many of us that failure is something to be avoided. Innovation, however, is almost always the result of a long string of failed attempts. Wanting and trying to be better is the mark of true innovators, and if you want to build a culture that not only supports innovation but lives and breathes it, you'll need to demonstrate:

- the ability to provide positive feedback surrounding ideas and participation

- the willingness to recognise contributions large and small

- the willingness to provide incentives for those who think outside of their assigned roles

- the willingness to promote (and even model) cross functional work habits.

> "I think it's wrong to refer to attempts as failures. They aren't failures. They are mistakes. We went out and tried a lot of different things with franchisees, and if they didn't sell, they were just mistakes."
>
> — Tom Potter, Founder, Eagle Boys

> "We're still evolving out of deeply entrenched council culture where that entrepreneurial innovative spirit wasn't maybe as accentuated, and people are learning that it's alright to do new things. So, I think one of our challenges, and the challenges for most companies, is to be able to culturally fail quickly, and fail cheaply."
>
> — Glen Babington,
> Executive Manager Infrastructure Services, Unitywater

How managers build resilient teams

Through developing discourse on the innovation focus, leaders can point teams in the direction of the kind of business practices that will improve efficiency and performance. Additionally, through winning hearts and minds with communication, everyone will enjoy higher levels of engagement.

At Royal Dutch Shell in the UK prior to the GFC, the workforce was recognised as highly engaged with the help of a mature internal communications function and staff video channels. The internal communications function was large and featured a team at the centre of each division (upstream and downstream) as well as an internal communications adviser located alongside each executive director. What was impressive about the executive directors was their willingness to drive and participate in innovative communication methods, such as videos as a means of communicating with their staff in other countries. There was an in-house television studio and team, and the executive directors were the first to suggest video newsletters not only to relay important information but also to illustrate with pictures new campaigns, safety updates, etc. and show what different teams were doing.

Shell placed as much emphasis on staff engagement as they did on public relations. Since they were involved with and participating in company achievements, employees wanted to do their best and were rewarded. Some of them got to attend exclusive meet and greets with the F1 drivers Shell was sponsoring. It was a highly connected and an extremely inclusive environment. This made it impossible not to see the connection between the highly motivated employees and the culture of participation. Stagnation was almost impossible; staff were encouraged to change roles every few years, and this meant that they were able to bring their experience and expertise to different teams and ensure fresh ideas. Shell also gave their employees a great deal of autonomy and flexibility: they could work from home or, indeed, anywhere there was a Wi-Fi signal – all that mattered was that the job was done well.

Management gave teams a sense of confidence, autonomy, and a connectedness with leadership. This allowed them to shrug off difficulties, knowing that they could count on support from every level of the organisation.

The kind of culture described above is replicable. However, building a resilient team takes some resilience on your part as well. At the heart of team resilience is fearless communication, and when you encourage open and honest communication at every level, it's virtually certain that you'll hear some things that will make you flinch. This should never hold you back. It pays to establish rules in this kind of forum around choosing respectful words as much as possible and acknowledging the value that everyone uniquely brings to the table. As a leader, it will sometimes be hard to hear what your employees are saying but it's an opportunity to get closer to them and build up the bank of trust.

It makes sense that resilient teams are a product of effective leadership. How leaders interact with staff substantially affects engagement levels, which, in turn, influences productivity and the company's bottom line. Leadership requires a sharp focus on engagement because in times of change, people need to know what is going on and where they stand from people they trust. Naturally, some will be better at leading engagement than others but using the tips below should ensure it remains a priority.

- **Coach managers and hold them accountable for engagement levels**

  The most influential people in your employees' professional lives are their direct line managers. Hold managers accountable for building engagement plans with their employees and tracking their progress. Ensure they continuously focus on emotionally charging their employees. Real change occurs at the grassroots level, but leaders need to set the tone from the top. Therefore, you should measure your managers' engagement strategies in the same way you measure performance in their other duties.

- **Set goals that are tangible and measurable**

  Context is crucial for big picture thinkers. That is why business leaders must make objectives meaningful to employees in terms of their day-to-day experiences. Where does the individual's objectives fit within the team goals and company goals? Weekly team meetings can (and should) include discussions focused on boosting or sustaining participation levels that will contribute towards goal achievement. Regular team temperature checks will give management a good idea of whether goal-setting is aiming too high or too low.

- **Find ways to connect with each employee**

  This might sound straightforward, but this isn't as simple as line managers taking the time to say good morning to their staff. It means being present and aware enough to see their team members as individuals, each with his or her own talents, problems and experiences. Every interaction with an employee has the potential to trigger a deeper engagement or innovation. If you are relying on discretionary effort given willingly, such as collaboration, innovation or problem solving, it is give and take. Your staff must first feel that you know something about their motivations and that they are trusted and valued for their contributions.

Why leaders can't stay quiet

When it comes to bad news or communicating during uncertainty, leaders will either rise to the occasion or consciously step down from their responsibility to speak up. When you witness leaders who believe that becoming absorbed in the business of making business, ignoring whispers and burying their head in the sand will fly when it comes to speculation about changes that impact the working lives their staff, be sure that their reluctance to communicate will cost them dearly. Staying quiet means they are enabling misinformation to flow and inform decision making, and it alienates people. It may also be the tipping point for a valued staff member, which might mean that someone the company would rather not lose might not come back to work tomorrow.

Communication is a natural and instinctual response, unless fear is attached to it. When line managers are afraid of saying the wrong thing, this is understandable; a verbal misstep could cost them their jobs or inflame a sensitive issue. Today, however, leadership requires not only the business nous that got you the position in the first place, but also highly attuned people skills. This means that, like it or not, leaders must be communicators, coaches and facilitators.

I urge you to start the dialogue and take the rumour mill off 'speculation overdrive'. This might mean coaching your line managers. However, you can start with tying messaging back to the company values. By giving other leaders the right information (not just what to say but how and when to say it), you'll have dramatically fewer rumours circulating.

Putting innovation on the company agenda

The decision to focus attention on, invest in and pursue a culture of innovation will demand that, sooner rather than later, you have a frank discussion with your top team and with staff. The way innovative leaders prepare for this announcement is:

Vision – Come to the meeting with an idea of what a more innovative organisation will look like. Paint a picture.

Convene – Introduce the innovation focus at your top team meeting. Topics to cover during this meeting should include the rationale behind the move and how it ties in with the direction of the company.

Discuss – Be prepared to discuss your vision, being sure to touch on areas of focus and impacts on business as usual. Acknowledge that change activities and projects will continue but that innovation is something new with unknown but exciting possibilities. Include change management and HR leaders in this discussion.

Concur – There should be agreement surrounding the initial key messages that will be given to teams in the focus areas. Consistency in terms of time and message is extremely important during these early stages, so be sure that there's widespread agreement when it comes to what the key messages are, how they are to be delivered, and when.

Authenticate – Subject messaging to an authenticity (or BS) test. Linking the innovation agenda to the organisation's vision is powerful, but it's not enough. Since it is often unclear exactly where a focus on innovation will lead, there are, at least initially, bound to be unanswered (and unanswerable) questions. Prepare for these questions so that you can provide thoughtful and authentic answers. Though you might not have all the answers, it's better to admit as much than to provide less-than-accurate answers based on incomplete or unavailable data. Personally commit to keep everybody informed and to respond to relevant feedback. Crucially, follow through on your promise to do so.

A connected workplace culture

Let me close this chapter with a note on communication. It is the most powerful tool at your disposal, and this is especially the case when transitioning to a business strategy focused on innovation.

From regular e-newsletters and videos to discussion boards, tweets and employee forums, the frequent use of employee engagement leads to organisation-wide connectivity. It drives social and cultural participation in company culture, and, if used effectively, it can help your vision and key messages resonate from the top to the bottom of the organisation. By personally and actively contributing to these channels, you'll form a tighter knit community with you at its centre. You can show positive aspects of your personality and share your thoughts on whatever topics are relevant, all the while making yourself more approachable. Every manager throughout your organisation should follow your lead in keeping communication channels open. Regular reviews of communication channels will help ensure that communication doesn't become stale or repetitive.

Technology-enabled communication channels are not there to replace face-to-face engagement; rather, they should be communication multipliers. Social media collaboration is the go-to method of communication for many of us, with its key benefits being speed of transmission and responses. It is most beneficial when social media is combined with face to face engagement. The latter is particularly powerful to facilitate questions and context setting and is particularly beneficial for establishing authenticity and intention. When it comes to innovation, clarity is the goal: clarity of message, clarity of intention, clarity of purpose, clarity of vision. In the context of the company culture, employees need to know what the vision for driving innovation in the business looks like, why it is important and how their individual roles can contribute to achieving it. RESONATE is at the centre of the 5-step method because it is crucial to take your teams along the innovation journey with you. Encourage questions and opportunities for discussions between leaders and teams.

"I have said many times that everyone must march to the same drum. This is one reason why communication between franchisor and franchisee must be clear, regular, understood by all parties and documented as having been exercised (i.e., everybody needs to sign off to show they received the message). By the same token, at the time I was there, we had a very open-book policy; no secrets, no stuff hidden around corners."

– Tom Potter, Founder, Eagle Boys

Case Study: Resonate

Great example: Tony Hsieh, CEO, Zappos

Why: Tony is known for creating an outstanding company culture with passionate and talented employees.

How: He treats people well and they tell their friends.

Details: Zappos is an online retailer, now a part of Amazon. Hsieh has positioned his team at the heart of the business, and culture has become even more important than their commitment to customer service. Inside the Zappos office is a nap room, a bowling alley, a petting zoo, and you might find employees singing karaoke. There are even interactive games that help new staff members remember the names of everybody in the office. All new employees are greeted with a four-week training program. At the end of the first week, they are offered $2,000 to quit (this offer stands until the end of their training). This ensures that Zappos employees are there because they really want to be.

Zappos hires most people at an entry level, and staff can access a range of courses. All staff are expected to make at least one improvement every week to illustrate the Zappos core values. Some of the company values are:

- Embrace and drive change.

- Be adventurous, creative and open-minded.

- Build a positive team and family spirit.

The moral: You don't need a separate set of customer values when your frontline staff are highly engaged. Your staff can be the best endorsement for the products and brand.

Roadblock: Wrong people, wrong job

Is there a belief that you don't have the right teams and the right skills in house or at hand to analyse, plan, execute, and measure innovation? Whether it be disruptive or incremental, product, process or service, it's time to look at your organisation's RESOURCE pool.

RISK   RELATE   RESONATE   **RESOURCE**   REVOLUTIONISE

CHAPTER 8:
RESOURCE

Solution: There have never been more resources available

A culture of innovation within your organisation may require a significant cultural shift. It demands giving a voice to people with diverse thinking (diverse in terms of knowledge, skills and perspectives gained through life experiences). If in-house resources don't appear to be sufficient to power your innovative initiative or agenda, there are many resources available outside your existing staff talent pool.

Capability

It's not easy to look objectively at your company and decide whether or not you have the right people with the rights skills to deliver innovative outcomes. This is the first step of RESOURCE, which examines the capability domain in your organisation. Understanding the resources that are available to you will drive your ability to take action.

When innovating, the best-case scenario is an under-utilised capability domain – one that possesses a deep vein of untapped potential. However, even if there is latent potential in your organisation, it is not always enough. If groundbreaking innovation is the goal, it may be necessary to explore resources external to your company.

In the same way that multichannel approaches work well in communication, using more than one innovation channel can help bridge skills and knowledge gaps, which will, in turn, mature not just an isolated hub, but your entire organisation's innovation capabilities. In this section, we'll explore the five most popular innovation channels: outsourcing, collaboration, networking, acquisitions, and upskilling.

1. Outsourcing

The last few decades have witnessed a big push to outsource customer service and IT departments, and it seems that organisations have caught the outsourcing bug. Many companies are now turning to third parties for help with innovating products and services or simply researching ideas. Outsourcing may be an expensive option, but, for many who go this route, it can result in quicker and more comprehensive idea generation. This in turn means a faster speed to market. As with all outsourcing, there are pros and cons. Access to expertise in different fields is always beneficial; however, ensure that your company owns any products of innovation (rather than the supplier) and that all phases of the design and development processes are in keeping with your broader company objectives. In other words, you want innovation to be fit for purpose, fit for your customers and able to be integrated with your operating model.

"We recently moved to a security system as a service rather than an in-house approach. Similar to most organisations, cyber security is one of our biggest risks. We chose a company to provide global security as a service model, and we have wrapped that around our IT technology and operations, and that's been a real win. It has given us a massive uplift in being secure from cyber-attacks across multiple technology environments."

– Geoff Wenborn, CIO, Origin Energy

2. Collaboration

Organisations who might lack some of the in-house resources they need to power innovation on their own are looking to collaboration as a powerful innovation tool. Provided the businesses involved are compatible, joint ventures can result in successful innovation projects. Separate companies can be formed specifically for the delivery of a project, or two companies can work together for the mutual benefit of access to new markets and distribution, as well as finance and technology. Naturally, the appeal of this approach is that risk shared is risk diminished. Forward-thinking organisations are finding more and more creative ways to collaborate. Take a look at the recent emergence of 'hackathons', which are a great way to get experts from outside your organisation to brainstorm ideas and access collective problem solving when time to market is a critical factor. They are successful because they leverage not only expertise from outside sources but creativity as well. This open source method of innovation has been a huge success story for many of the organisations that have gone this route. Hackathons, if properly leveraged, can provide businesses with access to the latest technologies and expertise beyond their own capabilities.

"How the oil and gas industry works best is often through joint ventures to get things started. In IT, for example, we work closely with our key service suppliers, and together we look at ideas around smart innovations and new services. There's a lot of synergy for us in working closely with new key partners."

– Geoff Wenborn, CIO, Origin Energy

Partnerships can also be 'open innovation', including external partners such as universities or research institutions. Many research institutions undertake successful research partnerships with businesses, providing a win-win situation. Government research organisations in particular are often keen to partner with businesses. It allows them to supplement funding via consultancy, collaborative research and licensing contracts.

> "CSIRO is very much a collaborator. We work with many businesses to translate research into innovative products. We have had a 25-year partnership with Boeing for that very reason."
>
> – Dr. Keith McLean, Director of Manufacturing, CSIRO Manufacturing

> "We have innovation labs, such as the Gurrowa Innovation Lab we launched in Melbourne in early August, where we are able to co-create with customers, partners, vendors and members of our innovation network. Rather than just focus on technology at Telstra, we bring our customers in and work with them to define problems, issues, and to co-create solutions."
>
> – Paul McManus, Executive Director and Head of Global Enterprise Mobility, Telstra

3. Networking with industry associations

A number of senior leaders I met during my research for this book happily revealed that they are members of groups that openly discuss innovation. Whether informal or formal, these gatherings provide opportunities to collaborate more broadly. They provide opportunities to talk about technology, projects, etc. across industries or across the same customer group where products do not compete. Networking with industry associations provides ample opportunities to make alliances and share what works and what doesn't. Out-of-industry events can be a great source of inspiration, and you might find collaboration or partnership opportunities – perhaps where you least expect them.

"Attend events in different industries to see if technologies or ideas are applicable. Go to an industry conference for a completely different domain. Form collaboration hubs. It's all about the way you think about delivering a service. For example, you don't need to buy a fridge; you just need to have the service of food being at 4 degrees."

– Dr. Elliot Duff, Acting Research Director, CSIRO

"We interact with industry bodies like PACIA (the Plastics and Chemicals Industry Association) to help bring businesses together."

– Dr. Keith McLean
Director of Manufacturing, CSIRO Manufacturing

4. Acquisitions

At least one part of your organisation is looking at new technologies, products or markets, and these aren't always easy to implement into a business without certain capabilities. A good strategy for companies like Google has been to acquire start-ups with different but complementary core capabilities.

Apart from the benefits of accessing new skills and business streams, mergers and acquisitions can have a very positive impact on employer brands and work cultures. In order to maintain healthy work cultures and for attraction and retention reasons, remember to tackle carefully the integration of roles. Even when there is widespread buy-in for a merger or acquisition, change management is paramount to helping smooth such transitions.

"Because the company has grown so rapidly through acquisition, there is real business sponsorship and support for us to take advantage of all the shifts in the technology paradigm. In IT, we want to get to the cloud; we want to get mobile; we want to take advantage of consumption-based models; we want to do better with analytics; and potentially spawn new technologies for energy service consumers. Origin can benefit from doing it at scale."

– Geoff Wenborn, CIO, Origin Energy

"Through collaboration, we successfully defined and identified targets for mergers and acquisitions and examined what integration would look like after these acquisitions. The effect this exercise had on employee motivation, engagement and the growth of our business was a great success story."

– Marcelo Bastos, Chief Operating Officer, MMG

5. Upskilling your staff

Upskilling may help address skills gaps in your existing workforce. It may take externals to come in to the organisation to lead this training. If you don't have the necessary technical skills, for example, to improve a process, you'll need to start training existing staff so they can better understand the business problem you need to solve and the approaches required to address it. Your teams should already be making incremental improvements as agreed to processes, products or services. Though this may not represent a massive leap forward in terms of innovation, a 'safe change' such as improvements to processes or products or trialling a new database for example, may be a less risky path to take. For these types of changes, conventional project management methodology may be most appropriate. The fewer unknowns there are in the equation, the more possible it will be to lean upon the PRINCE (projects in a controlled environment) project management standard. This is only really applicable when the outcome and all of the variables are known prior to implementation.

This is not the case with the drive to innovate. As we've discussed throughout this book, while we can plan for innovation, predicting its outcomes is difficult. In a corporate environment where there are existing structures, there should be an emphasis on learning and experimentation. This will result in unexpected outcomes, but there are ways to make your organisation more nimble and able to take advantage of these surprises in powerful ways. We'll look at a formal process to manage innovation in the next chapter.

Of course, innovation isn't just about freeing up your employees' minds to think in more creative ways. The kinds of thought processes that tend to produce more innovative results need to be nurtured. I acknowledge the age-old argument that creativity might not be teachable, but upskilling with a focus on innovation is not about teaching creativity; it's about unlocking creative potential, encouraging collaboration and positive action.

In practical terms this means considering the following :

- Empower your staff to think beyond their job descriptions and in terms of the company's key innovation principles.

- Ensure your staff understand that, no matter what their role, their contributions (especially in terms of innovation) are of value.

- Check that staff feel a sense of urgency (the time to start innovating is now).

- Provide staff with support that helps them cut through or navigate corporate politics to ensure their ideas and delivery plans are escalated.

- Communicate progress on projects from conception to result including ability to get traction, failures and success stories.

> "I have given up trying to micro manage project teams, particularly when it comes to telling them what and exactly how to do things. These days, I prefer to give them the project and the deadline, and all I ask for is something cool. That's what they deliver."
>
> – Dr. Elliot Duff, Acting Research Director, CSIRO

The right fit

Recent research has shown that a lack of skilled workers is one of the first issues companies face when trying to encourage innovation. This is often attributed to skills and knowledge gaps with existing staff. Additionally, there can also be productivity issues, disconnects in middle management, and widespread difficulties (for a variety of reasons) in keeping pace with the changing needs of your customers. This can make it seem as though your business is (or, perhaps more appropriately, your people are) not a good 'fit' for a culture of innovation.

> "A lesson I didn't learn fast enough was to hire people who would fit our culture. It's tough to discover some of the most highly qualified people you've hired may not be the best cultural fit. My point is this: knowing exactly what your corporate culture is will allow you to make better hires. Define your culture and then make job descriptions to fit that mould."
>
> – Tom Potter, Founder, Eagle Boys

However, it is my firm belief that you can't legitimately say that your people are unfit for your culture of innovation if *any* of the following are true:

1. Your employees lack clarity around their current roles, including expectations, consequences and rewards.

2. Members of your team lack concrete (or even abstract) information about what difference the application of innovative qualities could make to their individual roles (i.e., they lack precisely defined expected outcomes).

3. Staff members aren't close enough to your customers to understand how the supply chain works.

4. Employees lack clarity in terms of how their role fits within the company's vision for the future. Without this clarity, they have no idea what incremental or disruptive innovation on their part could achieve.

5. Staff have not seen innovative problem solving and associative thinking at work.

6. Having been rapped on the knuckles for challenging the status quo, staff have learned to keep new ideas to themselves.

7. Workers are not being paid competitively or in a way that attaches rewards to innovative behaviours.

8. Staff members, when asked to provide feedback, say that they are not being heard.

All of the above issues will significantly impede attempts to introduce innovation across the organisation. These issues *must* be addressed if innovation is to gain traction. At the very least, it should be apparent that the organisation is taking the necessary steps to address these grievances. With increased clarity, communication, and responsiveness, you can expect to see employee performance, morale, and connectivity increase. If you try to refocus your teams on ideation or thinking laterally without addressing these issues, any momentum you have built will quickly lose steam.

> "Staff members are often underestimated in terms of their ability to innovate. They just need the right motivation and exposure to the right conditions. We've done a fair bit of investment in leadership over the last 18 months, and what we're finding is that, to build innovation, you need particular individuals who have a bent towards questioning the status quo and an inquiring mind. In theory, everyone might be encouraged to be an innovator, but you've actually got to champion those people that have a natural bent towards it, and they may not be at the right authority levels. You've got to look out for them and make sure their ideas are heard quickly."

– Glen Babington,
Executive Manager Infrastructure Services, Unitywater

I truly believe in the ability of everyone to innovate under the right conditions. I also acknowledge that technical expertise requires more than just upskilling staff. It takes years of experience, familiarity with systems, understanding complexities, etc. to reach expert status. That is why innovation capability should be sourced from as broad a range of innovation channels as possible. It pays to be on the lookout for new technologies, products and markets, and these won't be simple to research, introduce and embed without some degree of external expertise.

> "Leverage your capability, but it needs to be market focused in terms of what the industry is doing and you forming a point of view and sharing that with the industry. Do this and you'll create a halo effect – you'll be seen as a thought leader, which will, in turn, help you attract and retain the right type of people, and build a profile in the market."

– Paul McManus,
Executive Director and Head of Global Enterprise Mobility, Telstra

"One of our barriers to innovation was expertise, so we did a couple of acquisitions and recruited the right talent. Then you look at the next evolution that you're about to embark on and say, "Okay, what do we need now in order to do this?" Because it doesn't matter how good you are; you don't know everything."

– Maxine Horne, CEO, Vita Group

Case Study: Resource

Great example: Chris Ridd, Managing Director, Xero

Why: Xero has taken the accounting world by storm in a few short years. They are a great example of a company that innovates through third-party partnerships.

How: A cloud-based accounting software firm, Xero has been on innovative companies' lists thanks to the improvements it provides to payroll functionality and tax management.

Details: With more than 250,000 paying customers, Xero has created significant partnerships. One of these is with Dropbox, which enables the storage and sharing of documents in one location, facilitating collaboration between accountants and their clients. Another is with Adobe, which integrates Document Cloud eSign services across Xero. This enables electronic signing and submission of tax documents, replacing the need to print, sign and post the documents.

The moral: When products are already successful, it pays to partner up to make the customer experience better or more convenient.

Roadblock: The organisation lacks a formal innovation process

There may have been various attempts at innovating but for one reason or another, an organisation has failed to get traction in terms of implementation. For some businesses, it is a case of getting organisation-wide co-operation.

RISK   RELATE   RESONATE   RESOURCE   **REVOLUTIONISE**

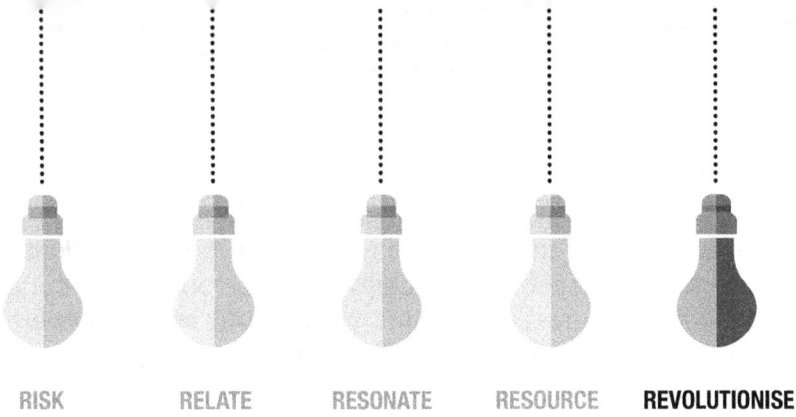

CHAPTER 9:
REVOLUTIONISE

This chapter features a significant contribution from
Dr. Wayne Hellmuth.

Solution: A formal innovation process is achievable and represents the culmination of the 5 R's

In this chapter, we examine three steps describing the REVOLUTIONISE process. The first step describes how to precisely define the business problem you want to solve. It's only once you are truly able to define and describe your problem that you will be able to produce an innovative product or process that solves it. Second, we will define the actual practice of designing innovative products. The final step of the innovation revolution process describes the development of the business model (i.e., how to develop strategies that allow you to monetise your newly developed innovative product).

The revolutionise process

Before we get into the technical side of this book, let's just re-visit the aim of this model: to achieve an enterprise-wide culture of innovation. Innovative pockets are fine but will not generate support across the business without all five steps. This chapter provides insight into key processes such as prototyping, the testing of business models and design thinking.

Design science is becoming a highly sought after skill in the corporate arena and the revolutionise process closely follows methods used in this field. Formal design science methods are geared towards research outcomes rather than business outcomes. Our model, therefore, has been adapted for lean business model practices.

The three major cycles or phases of our Revolutionise process are:

1. Relevance Cycle: understanding the customer's needs

2. Design Cycle: designing a novel product or process

3. Business Model Cycle: successfully bringing the product to market.

We can visualise the process in this way:

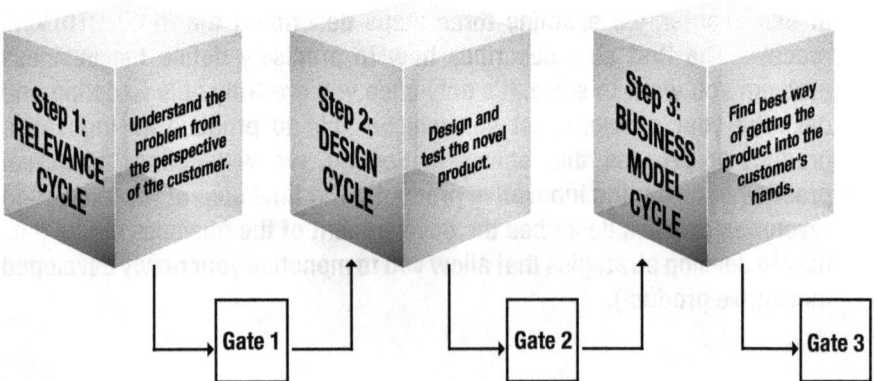

Step 1: RELEVANCE CYCLE — Understand the problem from the perspective of the customer.

Step 2: DESIGN CYCLE — Design and test the novel product.

Step 3: BUSINESS MODEL CYCLE — Find best way of getting the product into the customer's hands.

Gate 1 Gate 2 Gate 3

Figure 1: The Innovation Process

Figure 1 highlights the three steps of the process. Between each of the steps are gates or check points. These gates are there to ensure that each step has been thoroughly and properly completed. By following each step (and passing through each of the gates), you'll ensure that the innovative process is a highly efficient one.

Step 1 – Relevance Cycle

When it comes to innovation, understanding the actual business problems, or anticipating future business problems is difficult. This is the step that is so problematic for would-be innovators, and it is also the step that is least formalised within businesses.

We begin this chapter by dissecting and examining what makes a complex business problem – often referred to as 'wicked'. We use this term not in a traditional sense, but to denote the resistance of such problems to being resolved. Academics have invested considerable time describing the characteristics of wicked problems. These characteristics provide strong foundations for understanding solution-resistant barriers that the innovative leader will come up against. We begin this section by discussing why we struggle to define and deal with business problems.

Research has found that issues generally arise when there are multiple stakeholders within and external to an organisation, all with competing demands, perspectives, and ideas about what is needed to fix the particular business problems. These often-competing viewpoints are overlaid with subjective values that conceal the root of the problems. While it is up to the innovative leader to understand and find solutions to these problems, the thorny nature of wicked problems makes doing so one of (if not the) most difficult issues that innovators face. Solving one issue may create new issues elsewhere; some prove to be circular in nature, which leads to them being shelved rather than solved.

To truly revolutionise your organisation's approach to innovation, two barriers to problem solving must be broken through: problem complexity/human finitude and normative behaviours. Let's look at each of these in turn.

Problem complexity meets human finitude: A problem appears to be (or is actually) unsolvable with the human resources at hand.

When a problem is particularly complex, the vast majority of people will reach a saturation point – the point at which they are simply incapable of further deepening their understanding of the issue and its many facets. The short-term memory has, as research has shown, limited storage; the average person can hold a maximum of seven items (give or take) in his or her mind before the web begins to unravel. Thus, when the issue is a complex one—as wicked problems invariably are—there might, depending on the size of the company, only be a handful of individuals in the organisation who can truly grasp the matter at hand.

Studies conducted in the seventies on the problem-solving process found that "as decision complexity increases beyond [a certain] point, people become more conservative and apply more subjective criteria which are further and further removed from reality."[1] It's important to recognise that less-than-optimal outcomes are not the result of sloppiness or laziness or the inability of teams to work together; rather, they are the result of a crossed complexity threshold.

It is the role of leaders to find ways to first understand and then reduce complexity in ways that make allowance for human limitations. Innovation teams, for instance, should contain a wide range of skillsets and problem-solving approaches (sourcing from different departments is often a good way to ensure that the team is intellectually diverse). Short-term, cross-functional teams can also be a powerful way to create a web of understanding that approaches a particular problem from as many different perspectives as possible.

HP for example, has based their corporate culture on the integration and reinforcement of critical opposites. HP leadership believes that in order to maintain their competitive advantage, cross-functional teams are imperative. The kind of environment this creates might appear to be dichotomous, celebrating and supporting, as it does, individualism and teamwork simultaneously, but the company has found that

---

1 Filley, A, House, R & Kerr, S, *Managerial Process and Organizational Behavior*, (Glenview, IL: Scott, Foresman, 1976).

innovation and cross-functional partnerships frequently go hand in hand. They've further concreted this approach by rating their employees both on their participation in cross-functional teams and their personal achievements (expecting to see some balance between the two).

However, research presented in the *Harvard Business Review* has found that as much as 75 per cent of cross-functional teams were actually dysfunctional. It seems that these teams failed because they did not have clear governance structures, accountability, specific goals, and organisational support. The take-home message here is that if you are going to have cross-functional teams that attempt to tackle complex problems, assembling the team will not be enough. You'll need to support your teams and put clear governance structures in place.

Normative behaviours: approaches to innovation remain tethered to the status quo

Difficulties in initiating innovation and exploring new directions are rooted in established routines. People are conditioned, for the most part, to operate within the parameters of protecting and continuing existing operational practices, and this leads to organisational inertia and conformity. Our unwavering desire for consensus has made us excellent social and political animals, but it also makes us prone to in-group/out-group thinking and, at times, it turns us into irrationally defensive resisters who push back against anything that runs counter to established norms.

Innovation by definition disrupts the status quo, so you need to be prepared for resistance to change (we've discussed this in RESONATE). As a leader, the onus is on you to intervene and shift focus from routine to innovative activities. Remember that even innovative organisations are constantly managing to swim with the current rather than against it; the true innovators are those who constantly feed energy into the system in order to keep the momentum going. Once we have mobilised support for innovation, we can begin the innovation process in earnest by seeking to better understand the customer.

Understanding customers' problems

"You've got to start with the customer experience and work backwards for the technology. You can't start with the technology and try to figure out where you're going to try to sell it. I made this mistake probably more than anybody else in this room, and I've got the scar tissue to prove it. As we have tried to come up with a strategy and a vision for Apple, it started with, 'What incredible benefits can we give to the customer? Where can we take the customer?' not, 'Let's sit down with the engineers and figure out what awesome technology we have and then how are we going to market that.' I think that's the right path to take."

– Steve Jobs, Founder, Apple

"The pull model offers an opportunity to be creative. You create a relationship with a customer, and if you put the customer at the centre of everything you do, and you create that degree of trust, that customer will come to you to present their problems, which allows you to innovate with them, and that's probably the greatest opportunity to create offers or solutions or new business models that you may have never considered before."

– Paul McManus,
Executive Director and Head of Global Enterprise Mobility, Telstra

The most innovative companies demonstrate a belief in the power of customer insight. Regularly collecting data on customer behaviours and experiences is something that has become the bedrock of intelligent business practices. The more insights that can be collected and the broader the range of sources, the easier it becomes to determine statistical correlations between consumer behaviours. Passing through the Relevance Cycle means attention to trends and variability, which will allow your organisation to tailor offerings to demand.

Gate 1: Did you really understand the customer problem?

How do you know you have found and accurately described a customer problem? Before the decision is made to invest money into the next stage of developing an innovative product, you need to be quite certain that the innovation does, indeed, solve a customer problem. There are two tests designed to do just this that both need to be passed before moving on to the Design Cycle:

- The customer validation test – Speak with your customers and ask them whether you have really understood and defined their most important and pressing problem. Note, language standards are important when describing both the problem and solution. Following are some tips on structuring ways to communicate the customer problem and its potential solution:
    - Describe the parts (entities) that make up the problem.
    - Describe the relationship between the parts of the problem.
    - Describe the misaligned or missing parts of the problem and their relationships.
    - Validate the problem parts with multiple sources (multiple customers, suppliers, etc.).
- The relate test – Is what you communicate to the customer clearly resonating with the direction of their business and its immediate or anticipated requirements?

Step 2 – Design Cycle: design and product development

Following problem definition, and as long as you've taken steps to assure that the proposed solution directly addresses the needs of your customers, the next stage is the development of a prototype. There are four stages of prototyping:

1. A **Conceptual Prototype** is a conceptual representation of the innovation.

2. A **Proof-of-Principle Prototype** explores some, but not all, functional aspects of the intended design.

3. A **Visual Prototype** captures the size and appearance, but not the functionality, of the intended design.

4. A **Functional Prototype** captures both function and appearance of the intended design. In commercial organisations, the functional prototype should be minimalistic, but it should highlight the brilliance and potential of the new and innovative product.

We will illustrate each of the four prototyping stages with the following example:

An innovation project sought to improve data collection and data quality related to student learning in the classroom. In the first stage of design, researchers proposed a number of novel ideas. Each novel idea was presented back to the research team as a **Conceptual Prototype**. One conceptual prototype (shown in Figure 2) used a Bluetooth notification system to automate the look-up of student data based on the proximity of the teacher to the student.

Conceptual prototypes can be as simple as a single diagram.

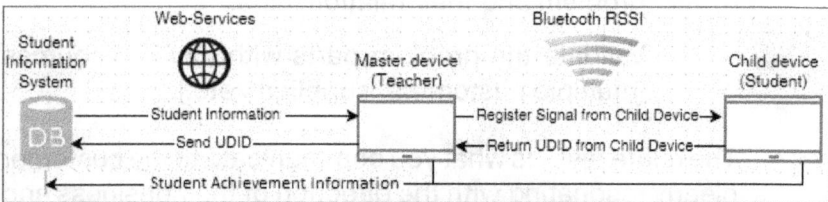

Figure 2: The Conceptual Prototype of the Bluetooth signal-based automated look-up function.

The feasibility of the Conceptual Prototype was first discussed and then accepted, and work began on the **Proof-of-Principle Prototype**. The Proof-of-Principle Prototype developed in this example tested the viability of the conceptual principle. Figure 3 shows the mobile device capturing multiple other mobile device IDs and their Received Signal Strength Indication (RSSI) strength. The conceptual principles of the innovation were proven with the use of a proof-of-principle prototype.

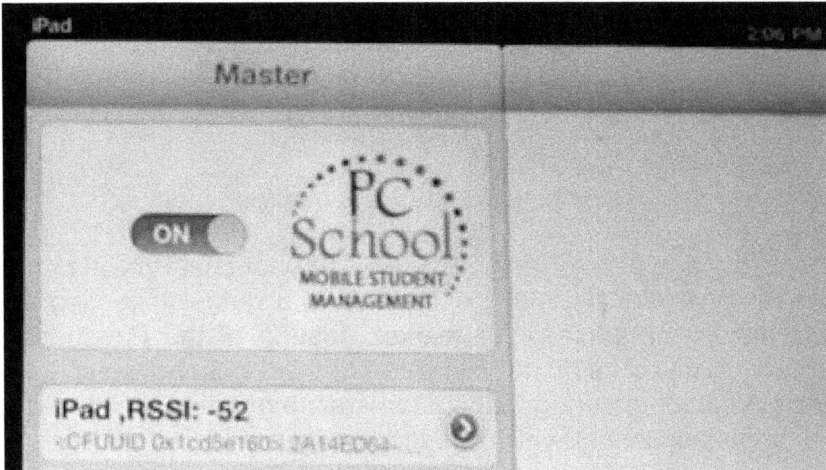

Figure 3: Proof-of-Principle Prototype

Effective innovation teams should be able to produce proof-of-principle prototypes relatively quickly. The Google glasses prototype, for example, was produced in less than three hours!

Given the success of the Proof-of-Principle Prototype, significant investment in time and resources were allocated to developing the **Visual Prototype**. The use of a wire-framing technique allowed something to be produced that gave an accurate representation of the look and feel of the mobile-based application containing the Conceptual Prototype. Not all design considerations could be represented in this prototype. Other considerations related to back-end infrastructure were carefully documented to ensure that the innovative application included all of the requirements listed in the design document (i.e., the requirements to realise the service strategy, enable business functions and to ensure the applications and technology layers had the correct functional design).

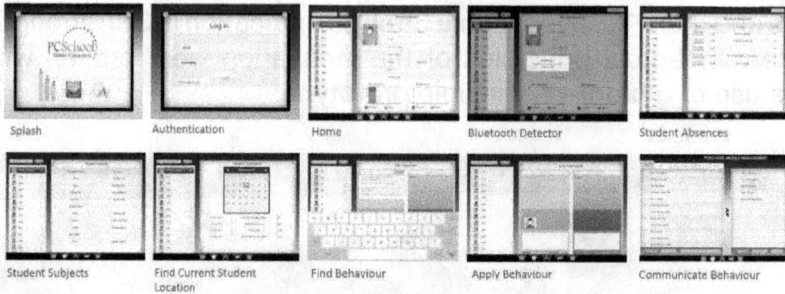

Splash Authentication Home Bluetooth Detector Student Absences

Student Subjects Find Current Student Location Find Behaviour Apply Behaviour Communicate Behaviour

Figure 4: The final design for the Visual Prototype.

The final stage of the Design Cycle was Functional Prototyping. The **Functional Prototype** was subjected to a range of testing to determine its readiness for market. Testing of the Functional Prototype falls outside of discussion of this book, however, this step is vital for ensuring that customers are not disappointed by the 'bugs' associated with your innovative product.

There are a number of advantages for staging your prototyping this way. A staged approach means that you are not investing money unnecessarily (i.e., into innovation projects beyond their staged success). The staged approach also allows your innovation teams to mature their thinking at each stage of development.

Gate 2: Testing the effectiveness of your prototype

With a prototype in hand, it is important that, before you take the product to market, you test its efficacy with your customers. We've arrived at the second gate, and there are a number of tests we'll need to pass before moving on to the third stage.

The WOW test: Do the customers love it?

You need to get a WOW from your customers when you present your prototype for the first time. It's what the board of directors will need to see if they are to dedicate the funds needed to move the product to the next stage in the development process.

The payment test: Are they willing to pay for it?

Present your product to multiple groups in order to trial with different price points. This will help you determine what the optimal price will be. When you present the prototype to your customers, you can, for example, tell your customers that pre-orders can be made and, based on these customers' appetites at each price point tested, you can settle on a price. Once you've done that, you can start to predict what your profits will be.

Step 3 – The Business Model Cycle: successfully bringing your product to market

Given that we know that the customer loves your innovation and is willing to pay for it, the business needs to develop a business model. It is essential to develop or rework your business model so that it can accommodate the innovation, which, of course, includes getting it to your customer base. An effective business model depends on developing and refining three important attributes:

1. finding high-value customers (those who are easy to locate, want the product/service, and will pay a good price for it). Every product has a customer 'sweet spot'. In the example of a Gold Coast tourism operator, young Japanese couples were the high-value customers. With a globally connected market, you no longer need to limit yourself to your immediate surroundings. If something doesn't fit with local tastes or cultures, it might find a receptive audience elsewhere, but this should have been established by now!

2. offering significant value to customers (benefits such as faster, better quality, cheaper price, etc.)

3. delivering significant margins (achieved by improving processes, greater efficiency in distribution channel, etc.).

There are a number of ways to create new business models with your top team or leaders. A Business Model Canvas, pioneered by Alexander Osterwalder, can be used to help companies begin to explore the most appropriate business model for their products and services. The Business Model Canvas, at its simplest, is a pre-formatted template for documenting and developing new business models. It is a tool for exploring value proposition, infrastructure, customers, and price-points for the new innovative product or service that pays particularly close attention to trade-offs. Teams can use the canvas to test a proposed business model by building a prototype of a new model with the help of sticky notes. Many ideas for new or revised business models are explored in this way.

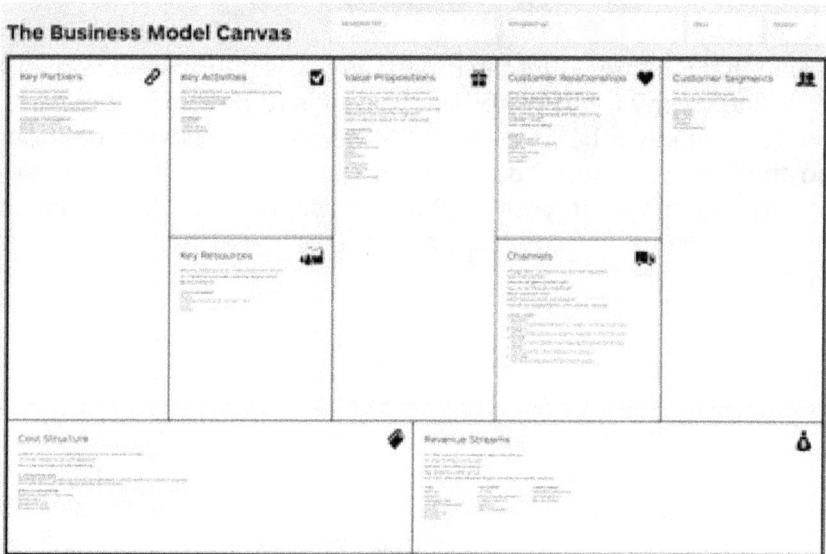

Figure 5: Example of Business Model Canvas.

When we examine businesses such as Uber and Netflix, who first went to market with a product that wasn't exactly novel, it is generally accepted that the renewed success of these companies is related to their changing business models. While Uber's business model offers new value to customers (benefits such as faster, better quality, cheaper price), Netflix's business model offers an improved efficiency in distribution channel, etc. The important thing to note about innovation is that it is *not* just about understanding the customer or the process of designing new products. The Innovation Revolution Stage is the process of undertaking all three of the development cycles mentioned in this chapter: understanding the customer, design, and producing the best business model.

Gate 3: Testing the effectiveness of your business model

The final gate of the innovation method is testing the validity of your business model. To find out whether or not your proposed business model will be profitable and sustainable, you'll need to administer two tests:

Customer satisfaction (value test)

This test can be completed with the aid of simple surveys or direct customer feedback. The purpose of this test is to determine if the customer sees the product as a good buy. Be specific with your questions. Remember, the customer may value things about your product or your business model that were not intended as selling features. Specific and open-ended questions will help you capture the specifics about what the customer likes about your new innovative product.

Customer referral test

The car service Uber, for example, gives you a free ride for every referral of their Uber app. The ultimate product sells itself. If you can go one step further and get your customers to promote your product on your behalf, you know you are riding a winner.

The design thinking mindset

Associative or design thinking is more than a process – it is a mindset. Organisations are experimenting with it more as an important part of reframing and solving problems because the design thinker makes connections without constraints. A design scientist is trained to be aware of thinking practices that limit creative solutions. Thinking can be constrained by culture, prejudices, personal motivation and experiences. For example, Carl Jung, the Swiss psychiatrist and philosopher, noted that much of Western thinking is dialectical in nature: good and bad; black and white; right and wrong. This way of thinking helps the thinker skirt the many issues that complexity presents. This type of binary thinking is utterly pervasive, and it profoundly affects the way we understand (or do not understand) and cope (or do not cope) with complex problems.

Einstein famously stated, "We can't solve problems by using the same kind of thinking we used when we created them". Most people are unaware of the approach they use when they are defining or understanding problems. A design scientist is trained to understand and recognise the biases and methods that are attached to both problem creation and, subsequently, problem solving as well.

Design thinking draws on:

- imagination

- intuition

- logic

- reasoning

- research

- a focus on outcomes (producing a result for the customer).

How to incorporate design thinking into your work life

Design thinking is a process that includes the 'building' of ideas, with few, or no, constraints to design possibilities. An example of a design thinking exercise that has none of these constraints is the orthogonal exercise. Orthogonal means right angles. For example, what would be right angles to 'black and white'? Answers may include 'midday' or 'negotiable'.

Design thinking can consist of a number of various types of thinking such as analysis and synthesis, convergent and divergent thinking. Analysis for example is a Greek term for 'pulling apart'. We use analysis to define the problem into its various parts or components so that they may be examined individually. Synthesis is used to build or put back together. Once we have broken our problem into parts, we can synthesise how to put the parts back together in a more desirable form.

We use divergent thinking when we brainstorm. This is a method that is used to come up with as many possible solutions to problems as possible. Conversely, convergent thinking is a way to eliminate possible designs and to narrow in on a solution to the defined problem.

In Summary

This chapter presented the three cycles to revolutionising your business through innovation. The first stage of the innovation process required that the innovative leader be an expert in both the customers and their problems. We emphasised the importance of this stage in the innovation process. Using multiple sources and perspectives in defining the customer problem will ensure you have all the information that you need to move to the design cycle. Make sure you check with your customers that you have fully understood the problem.

The second stage of innovation (the design stage) can be extremely rewarding, but it can also be frustrating at times. If done well, your employees will be the ones eager to get to work each day to make a difference. As we mentioned, cross-functional teams can produce some great ideas; however, without clear goals, the design process can be very frustrating. Without governance structures, long-term collaboration between departments can be inhibited. Good working relationships are vital if you want to produce novel solutions.

The final stage of the innovation process is the development of the business model. The business model is key to getting great products into the hands of your customers. There have been some wonderful inventions made that the general public has never heard of. By following the tests that have been provided for you in this chapter, you will prevent yourself from spending time and money on a new product or process for which customers have no appetite.

Case study: Revolutionise

Great example: Australian Wedding Dress Company

Why: Capitalised on an emerging market using the company's existing resources.

How: Used all five Rs of the Innovation Accelerator and disrupted a local tourism market.

Details: A Gold Coast wedding dressmaker was struggling to make profits. The percentage of Australian couples at 'marriage age' was decreasing, and local competition in the wedding dress market had increased. His problem was compounded by the fact that he had heavily invested in making a large range of custom handmade dresses. The forecast for future business was not good; however, closing the business with such an investment in wedding dress stock simply was not an option.

Through market analysis, the owner of the business determined that he needed to drastically change his business model to increase his market share. Through brainstorming, he had a crazy idea. His imaginative idea was to sell the experience of the Western-style wedding to the Japanese.

Japanese tourism in Australia was at its peak. Around this time, the Prince and the soon-to-be Princess of Japan were planning their wedding. The opportunity presented itself. He flew to Japan to convince the royal couple to have a Western-style wedding. The deal came with the promise of putting the bride in a dress covered with four million dollars' worth of diamonds. The event was one of the most watched events ever seen on Japanese television. Thanks to successful partnerships with key internal Japanese tourism booking agents, a completely new and highly successful business blossomed. The idea was imaginative, but it was backed by research, good timing, ideal market conditions and an understanding of Japanese culture.

The design of the Australian Wedding Experience was built to be like the very popular royal experience. It included Rolls Royce transfers, helicopter flights over the Great Barrier Reef and even cuddles with koalas. All of these experiences were accompanied with glamour photography. The young Japanese couples spent an average of $5,400 per wedding!

This new business model was not popular with local business owners, who relied heavily on Japanese tourism. The wedding dress business was now also a limousine company, tourism company and photography house. They were unstoppable.

The moral: An innovative leader must always be aware of prevailing and facilitating market conditions. Then it is a matter of rising to the challenge of creating and fostering supportive environments for the incubation and development of innovation. One way to do this is to remove any barriers that may constrain employees' participation in activities that will (or might) improve company outputs in the form of innovation. Remember, the window of success for an innovation may only be open for a brief moment. Therefore, it pays to ensure participants are proactive and ready to take the opportunities when they are presented. Employees need to have the right mindset; they need to be comfortable operating in ambiguity and prepared to act on opportunities when they arise.

CONCLUSION:
The Destination

Picture yourself once again in the audience at the Innovation Show. It's another awards night, but this time you hear your name called alongside several others from your organisation. You walk up on stage together, exchanging smiles with your colleagues as you accept your awards. This almighty team has created an industry-changing innovation. In the front row of the audience you see your biggest competitor and smiling, they give you a wave. This is the moment you have fought for and earned. Your resolve has placed you centre stage at the innovation show.

Truly remarkable achievements are possible beyond the current state of your business. Whether you look at innovation from a business model sustainability perspective, a people perspective, or a proximity to your customers' perspective, innovation makes perfect sense. There are only upsides to making it an integral part of your workplace.

Everyone has a role to play in an innovation culture, from the individual who thinks about better ways to complete a task to those who put ideas forward or track attempts and failures. Though implementing a culture of innovation may not translate to industry-disrupting change, it will make your business more sustainable, profitable, and more attractive to your customers and employees. Being part of the innovation process keeps the culture alive and brimming with possibilities.

Remember the five Rs, which will help keep you on the road to innovation:

- Risk
- Resonate
- Relate
- Resource
- Revolutionise.

Finally, keep in mind that at the heart of all five of these are your people and your customers.

The end game: what an innovative culture looks like

If you want to know whether your organisation is making strides towards a more innovative future, there are eight things you should hope to see:

1. Leaders have clarity about and communicate both the vision and innovation's place in it

You and your top team have a clear vision for the future of the organisation. Team leaders and managers understand that to be an innovative organisation means that innovation must be encouraged and part of the company fabric. Business leaders prioritise innovation projects, reporting failures and successes alike. Deep engagement and powerful communication are commonplace.

2. There is a formal process for innovation and an innovation plan

Everyone understands the innovation process, plan and the rules for idea assessment and management. This is supported by leadership acknowledgment and feedback, which is clear and timely.

3. Problem solving and idea creation are part of every role

Employees know what their roles are and are encouraged to share ideas for local and enterprise improvements. This may mean allocated time during which employees are encouraged or even expected to break from routine roles or join cross-functional project teams. For some organisations, this is done weekly; for others it is less frequent, but it's not so much about how much time is invested as it is about the time spent being productive in terms of results and fresh ideas.

4. Ideas are encouraged and implemented quickly

There is a positive energy in the workplace because ideas are being implemented and your leadership team is helping to drive this momentum. Leaders are using design thinking techniques with their teams.

5. Collaboration with externals is part of the norm

Your staff and customers are more knowledgeable because you are keeping them informed with expertise you are gaining from partners, experts, and specialists. This collaboration with externals is also exposing your people to new industries and different ways of thinking about problems.

6. It is a great place to work

Attraction and retention are not key business problems. Staff feel themselves to be part of the organisation and are actively contributing to its growth.

7. There is tracking and measuring in place

Successes and failures are measured, recognised, rewarded and communicated.

8. You're not standing still

Rather than seeking out comfort, the organisation is actively seeking new territories and innovative direction. From top to bottom, everybody understands that innovation is the surest way to keep the organisation focused on (and moving toward) a prosperous future.

Start innovating

We started out at the beginning of this book by discussing innovation as a repeatable process using the 5-step method. Combining these steps will open up a door to a world of possibilities. You can look forward to being more competitive because your business will move in tandem with customer demand guided by expert insight. Growth will spur your organisation to new heights. It will enjoy an increased industry profile and, of course, more profits as well. Your highly motivated workforce will follow your vision and feel inspired to contribute to the organisation's ongoing success.

We've reached the end of this journey together, and now it's time to put the plan into action. This book should serve as a roadmap, giving you the guidance and the tools you need to step forward on the path with confidence. Along the way, you've heard what the experts have had to say, and, I hope, you're now driven by a passion to start innovating in earnest.

> "You know, I think a lot of times I've made decisions and people have said, 'Based on what?' I said, 'I don't know. It just felt right'."
>
> — Maxine Horne, CEO, Vita Group

AFTERWORD:
On Self-Care and Care for Others

CEOs, senior leaders and middle managers may not get a lot of sympathy for all the stress and hard work that goes into running a company. While an executive salary is a big draw card, chances are, you are in this role for more than money. Still, the magnitude of responsibility (self-imposed or not) can take a toll on your health.

Work-life balance is something we all strive for. Leaders understand the importance of striking this balance in their own lives, but the best ones also know that it is their responsibility to give their employees the opportunity to strike that very same balance. My challenge to you is to check that your people are given the direction they need to complete their work within the expected time and that this doesn't eat into their much-needed personal time. If employees are frequently or constantly staying back to complete work, they either have too much on their plates (which is stressful and unhealthy over a long period of time), they have a deadline to meet (in which case occasional longer hours may make sense), or they are trying to impress someone (and that someone might be you).

There is a difference between going above and beyond to deliver for a company and sitting in a seat to accumulate hours in the hope that the boss will be impressed by studiousness. Wise leaders understand that employees need direction, recognition, trust and respect. Equally as important is balance, which must be achieved if staff are to prosper and grow, and help the organisation to do the same. Attempting to please a clock-watching boss by warming a seat after hours often represents a compromise of personal values (and often corporate ones as well). As a leader, you are well placed to set the standards not only in terms of the performance of your employees but their well-being as well.

The kind of behaviours you model when it comes to managing pressure and stress, as well as balancing personal and professional life, says a great deal about what you expect of your employees and what they should, therefore, expect of themselves. How you handle bad news, good news, change, and daily operational discussions will tangibly influence how your employees do the same.

The same goes for letting your employees see what kind of person you are outside of your office or the boardroom. This need not cross privacy boundaries, but provides more of an insight into your values. I once worked with a CEO who, despite working long hours, attended weekly exercise bootcamp sessions held for staff before work. The CEO's participation in a healthy staff activity made it clear that the organisational values he advocated (in this case, employee health and wellness) were not just for show. It was utterly transparent that these things were important to him on a deeply personal level, and to demonstrate this, he placed himself on an equal footing with his employees. He spoke about the value of exercise as a good way to keep fit and manage pressure and something that – with a bit of planning and encouragement – could be integrated into even the busiest of daily routines. This was a leader who knew the value of self-care and who understood the importance of practicing what you preach.

As an influencer, you absolutely need to take care of yourself, but you also need to be *seen* taking care of yourself. Walking the talk of self-care in this way will make a world of difference to those whom you influence.

"The top CEOs are those who've learned to balance their lives, take care of their health, manage their diet, develop good habits, pursue passions outside their work and avoid addictions of any kind."

– Tom Potter, Founder, Eagle Boys

ABOUT THE AUTHOR

Tracy Walsh is passionate about changing workforce cultures for the better for sustainability and growth. She has worked as a trusted adviser to CEOs and senior leaders in the UK, Europe and Australia over the past 22 years. Having held senior project and management roles, Tracy has provided strategic engagement advice to organisations such as Royal Dutch Shell, AXA Insurance, Schroders' Investment Bank, Royal Bank of Scotland, Rio Tinto, BMA Coal, Energex and government departments such as the UK and Queensland Departments of Education. Her enterprise-wide engagement strategies and delivery plans have been designed to align major changes with informed stakeholders. Through connecting all levels of organisations with change events, she has taught leaders how to drive the innovation agenda, including shifting cultural beliefs, boosting productivity and lifting morale.

Tracy's reputation has been built on thinking outside the square to assist leaders to deliver strategies for engagement, analyse roadblocks and put in place the foundations for innovation to thrive. Her theories have been endorsed by prominent CEOs and senior executives, as well as a broad community of innovators.

CONSULTING

Tracy Walsh is the CEO of Corporate Innovations Australia and consults with corporates and government departments to help leaders solve key business problems. **For a full list of programs and services, visit www.ciagroup.com.au**

THE INNOVATION ACCELERATOR PROGRAM

On the basis of this book, Tracy has developed **Innovation Accelerator** – designed to help CEOs implement the key themes of the 5-step method for growth and sustainability. It consists of a leadership training program for executives and middle managers. The face-to-face program is delivered in the offices of the client and has been successful the world over. The process is fast paced and results oriented, putting in place the fundamental requirements for an innovation-focused organisation.

Tailored to the nuances of business as well as government organisations, the course content has been created in conjunction with leading scientists, design thinkers and consultants. As industry thought leaders, they have had great successes in bringing breakthrough innovations to market. They stand behind Tracy Walsh's groundbreaking and holistic 5-step model as a program that helps organisations create and embed a culture of innovation.

Implement the 5-step method in your business. Arrange a consultation at www.ciagroup.com.au